W9-BYU-341

The
Bay Psalm Book

A FACSIMILE

REPRINT OF THE FIRST EDITION

OF 1640

36212

THE UNIVERSITY OF CHICAGO PRESS

Library of Congress Catalog Number: 56-5128

PRINTED BY THE MERIDEN GRAVURE CO.
MERIDEN, CONNECTICUT

Contents

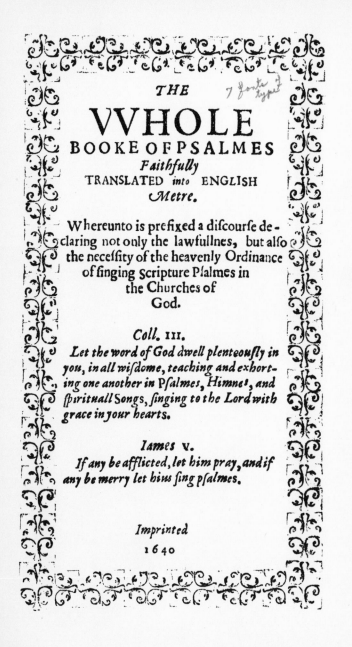

THE

VVHOLE

BOOKE OF PSALMES

Faithfully

TRANSLATED *into* ENGLISH

Metre.

Whereunto is prefixed a difcourfe de-
claring not only the lawfullnes, but alfo
the neceffity of the heavenly Ordinance
of finging Scripture Pfalmes in
the Churches of
God.

Coll. III.

*Let the word of God dwell plenteoufly in
you, in all wifdome, teaching and exhort-
ing one another in Pfalmes, Himnes, and
fpirituall Songs, finging to the Lord with
grace in your hearts.*

Iames V.

*If any be afflicted, let him pray, and if
any be merry let him fing pfalmes.*

Imprinted
1 6 40

The Preface.

THe singing of Psalmes, though it breath forth nothing but holy harmony, and melody : yet such is the subtilty of the enemie, and the enmity of our nature against the Lord, & his wayes, that our hearts can finde matter of discord in this harmony, and crotchets of division in this holy melody .-for- There have been three questiõs especially stirrĩg cõcerning singing. First. what psalmes are to be sung in churches? whether Davids and other scripture psalmes, or the psalmes invented by the gifts of godly men in every age of the church. Secondly, if scripture psalmes, whether in their owne words, or in such meter as english poetry is wont to run in? Thirdly. by whom are they to be sung? whether by the whole churches together with their voices? or by one man singing alõe and the rest joynĩg in silẽce, & in the close sayĩg amen.

Touching the first, certainly the singing of Davids psalmes was an acceptable worship of God, not only in his owne, but in succeeding times. as in Solomons time *2 Chron.* 5. 13. in Iehosaphats time *2 chron.* 20. 21. in Ezra his time *Ezra* 3. 10, 11. and the text is evident in Hezekiahs time they are commanded to sing praise in the words of David and Asaph, *2 chron.* 29, 30. which one place may serve to resolve two of the questions (the first and the last) at once. for this commandement was it cerimoniall

moniall or morall? some things in it indeed were cerimoniall, as their musicall instruments &c but what cerimony was there in singing prayse with the words of David and Asaph? what if David was a type of Christ, was Asaph also? was every thing of David typicall? are his words (which are of morall, universall, and perpetuall authority in all nations and ages.) are they typicall? what type can be imagined in making use of his songs to prayse the Lord? If they were typicall because the cerimony of musicall instruments was joyned with them, then their prayers were also typicall, because they had that ceremony of incense admixt with them: but wee know that prayer then was a morall duty, notwithstanding the incense; and soe singing those psalmes notwithstanding their musicall instruments. Beside, that which was typicall (as that they were sung with musicall instruments, by the twenty-foure orders of Priests and Levites. 1 *chron* 2 5. 9.) must have the morall and spirituall accomplishment in the new Testament, in all the Churches of the Saints principally, who are made kings & priests *Reu*. 1. 6. and are the first fruits unto God. *Reu*.14 4. as the Levites were *Num*. 3. 45. with hearts & lippes, in stead of musicall instruments, to prayse the Lord; who are set forth (as some iudiciously thinke) *Reu*.4. 4. by twenty foure Elders, in the ripe age of the Church, *Gal*.4. 1, 2, 3. answering to the twenty foure orders of Priests and Levites 1 *chron*. 25. 9.   Therefore not some select members

Preface.

members, but the whole Church is commaund-
ed to teach one another in all the severall sorts
of Davids psalmes, some being called by himselfe
מִזְמוֹרִים : psalms, some תְּהִלִּים : Hymns
some שִׁירִים : spirituall songs. soe that if the
singing Davids psalmes be a morall duty & ther-
fore perpetuall; then wee under the new Testamēt
are bound to sing them as well as they under the
old : and if wee are expresly commanded to sing
Psalmes, Hymnes, and spirituall songs, then either
wee must sing Davids psalmes, or else may affirm
they are not spirituall songs: which being penned
by an extraordīary gift of the Spirit, for the sake
especially of Gods spirituall Israell; not to be
read and preached only (as other parts of holy
writ) but to be sung also, they are therefore most
spirituall, and still to be sung of all the Israell of
God : and verily as their sin is exceeding great,
who will allow Davids psalmes (as other scrip-
tures) to be read in churches (which is one end)
but not to be preached also, (which is another end
soe their sin is crying before God, who will allow them to be read and preached, but seeke to
deprive the Lord of the glory of the third end of
them, which is to sing them in christian churches.
obj. 1 If it be sayd that the Saints in the primitive Church did compile spirituall songs of their
owne inditing, and sing them before the Church.
1Cor. 14, 15, 16.
Ans. We answer first, that those Saints compiled
these spirituall songs by the extraordinary gifts of

the

the spirit (common in those dayes) whereby they were inabled to praise the Lord in strange tongues, wherin learned *Paræus* proves those psalmes were uttered, in his Commēt on that place *uers* 14 which extraordinary gifts, if they were still in the Churches, wee should allow them the like liberty now. Secondly, suppose those psalmes were sung by an ordinary gift (which wee suppose cannot be evicted) doth it therefore follow that they did not, & that we ought not to sing Davids psalmes? must the ordinary gifts of a private man quench the spirit still speaking to us by the extraordinary gifts of his servant David? there is not the least foot-step of example, or precept, or colour reason for such a bold practise.

obj. 2. Ministers are allowed to pray conceived prayers, and why not to sing conceived psalmes ? must wee not sing in the spirit as well as pray in the spirit ?

Ans. First because every good minister hath not a gift of spirituall poetry to compose extemporary psalmes as he hath of prayer. Secondly. Suppose he had, yet seeing psalmes are to be sung by a joynt consent and harmony of all the Church in heart and voyce (as wee shall prove) this cannot be done except he that composeth a psalme, bringeth into the Church set formes of psalmes of his owne invētion; for which wee finde no warrant or president in any ordinary officers of the Church throughout the sciptures. Thirdly. Because the booke of psalmes is so compleat a System of

psalmes

pſalmes, which the Holy-Ghoſt himſelfe in infin-
ite wiſdome hath made to ſuit all the conditions,
neceſſityes, temptations, affections, &c. of men
in all ages; (as moſt of all our interpreters on the
pſalmes have fully and perticularly cleared)there
fore by this the Lord ſeemeth to ſtoppe all mens
mouths and mindes ordinarily to compile or
ſing any other pſalmes (under colour that the
ocaſions and conditions of the Church are new)
&c. for the publick uſe of the Church, ſeing, let
our condition be what it will, the Lord himſelfe
hath ſupplyed us with farre better; and therefore
in Hezekiahs time, though doubtleſſe there were
among them thoſe which had extraoridnary gifts
to compile new ſongs on thoſe new ocaſions, as
Iſaiah and Micah &c. yet wee read that they are
commanded to ſing in the words of David and
Aſaph, which were ordinarily to be uſed in the
publick worſhip of God: and wee doubt not but
thoſe that are wiſe will eaſily ſee; that thoſe
ſet formes of pſalmes of Gods owne appoynt-
ment not of mans conceived gift or humane
impoſition were ſung in the Spirit by thoſe holy Levites, as well as their prayers were in
the ſpirit which themſelves conceived, the
Lord not then binding them therin to any
ſet formes ; and ſhall ſet formes of pſalmes
appoynted of God not be ſung in the ſpirit now,
which others did then ?

Queſton. But why may not one cōpoſe a pſalme
& ſing it alone with a loud voice & the reſt joyne
with

with him in silence and in the end say **Amen?**
Ans. If such a practise was found in the Church
of Corinth, when any had a psalme suggested by
an extraordinary gift; yet in singing ordinary
psalmes the whole Church is to ioyne together
in heart and voyce to prayse the Lord. -for-
First. Davids psalmes as hath beene shewed,
were sung in heart and voyce together by the
twenty foure orders of the musicians of the Tem
ple, who typed out the twenty foure Elders all
the members especially of christian Churches *Rev*
5. 8. who are made Kings and Priests to God
to prayse him as they did : for if there were
any other order of singing Choristers beside
the body of the people to succeed those, the
Lord would doubtlesse have given direction
in the gospell for their quallification, election,
maintainance &c. as he did for the musicians of
the Temple, and as his faithfullnes hath done for
all other church officers in the new Testament.

Secondly. Others beside the Levites (the chiefe
Singers) in the Iewish Church did also sing the
Lords songs; else why are they commanded frequently to sing: as in psf. 100, 1, 2, 3. psf. 95, 1, 2, 3.
psf. 102. title. with vers 18. & *Ex.* 15. 1. not only
Moses but all Israell sang that song, they spake
saying (as it is in the *orig.*) all as well as Moses,
the women also as well as the men. v. 20 21. and
deut. 32. (whereto some thinke, Iohn had refer-
ence as well as to *Ex.* 15. 1. when he brings in the
protestant Churches getting the victory over the
Beast

Beaſt with harps in their hands and ſinging the ſong of Moſes. *Reu.* 15. 3.) this ſong Moſes is commanded not only to put it into their hearts but into their mouths alſo: *deut.* 31. 19. which argues, they were with their mouths to ſing it together as well as with their hearts.

Thirdly. Iſaiah foretells in the dayes of the new-Teſtament that Gods watchmen and deſolate loſt ſoules, (ſignified by waſt places) ſhould with their voices ſing together, *Iſa.* 52. 8, 9. and *Reu.* 7. 9, 10. the ſong of the Lamb was by many together, and the Apoſtle expreſly commands the ſinging of Pſalmes, Himnes, &c. not to any ſelect chriſtians, but to the whole Church *Eph.* 5. 19 *coll.* 3. 16. Paule & Silas ſang together in private *Acts.* 16. 25. and muſt the publick heare ōly one man ſing? to all theſe wee may adde the practiſe of the primitive Churches; the teſtimony of ancient and holy *Baſil* is in ſtead of many *Epiſt.* 63 When one of us (ſaith he) hath begun a pſalme, the reſt of us ſet in to ſing with him, all of us with one heart and one voyce; and this ſaith he is the common practiſe of the Churches in Egypt, Lybia, Thebes, Paleſtina, Syria and thoſe that dwell on Euphrates, and generally every where, where ſinging of pſalmes is of any account. To the ſame purpoſe alſo *Euſebius* gives witnes, *Eccleſ. Hiſt. lib. 2. cap.* 17. The objections made againſt this doe moſt of them plead againſt joyning to ſing in heart as well as in voyce, as that by this meanes others out of the Church will ſing

**   as

as also that wee are not alway in a sutable estate to the matter sung, & likewise that all cannot sing with understanding ; shall not therefore all that have understanding ioyne in heart and voyce to - gether ? are not all the creatures in heaven, earth, seas : men, beasts, fishes, foules &c. commanded to praise the Lord, and yet none of these but men, and godly men too , can doe it with spirituall understanding ?

As for the scruple that some take at the trans- latiō of the book of psalmes into meeter, because Davids psalmes were sung in his owne words without meeter : wee answer. First. There are many verses together in several psalmes of David which run in rithmes (as those that know the heb- rew and as Buxtorf shews *Thesau.* pa. 629.) which shews at least the lawfullnes of singing psalmes in english rithmes .

Secondly. The psalmes are penned in such verses as are sutable to the poetry of the hebrew language , and not in the common style of such other bookes of the old Testament as are not poeticall ; now no protestant doubteth but that all the bookes of the scripture should by Gods ordinance be extant in the mother tongue of each nation, that they may be understood of all, hence the psalmes are to be translated into our eng- lish tongue; and if in our english tongue wee are to sing them, then as all our english songs (accord ing to the course of our english poetry) do run in metre, soe ought Davids psalmes to be translated

into

into meeter, that soe wee may sing the Lords songs, as in our english tongue soe in such verses as are familiar to an english eare which are commonly metricall : and as it can be no just offence to any good conscience to sing Davids hebrew songs in english words, soe neither to sing his poeticall verses in english poeticall metre : men might as well stumble at singing the hebrew psalmes in our english tunes (and not in the hebrew tunes) as at singing them in english meeter, (which are our verses) and not in such verses as are generally used by David according to the poetry of the hebrew language : but the truth is, as the Lord hath hid from us the hebrew tunes, lest wee should think our selves bound to imitate them; soe also the course and frame (for the most part) of their hebrew poetry, that wee might not think our selves bound to imitate that , but that every nation without scruple might follow as the graver sort of tunes of their owne country songs , soe the graver sort of verses of their owne country poetry.

Neither let any think, that for the meetre sake wee have taken liberty or poeticall licence to depart from the true and proper sence of Davids words in the hebrew verses, noe; but it hath beene one part of our religious care and faithfull indeavour, to keepe close to the originall text.

As for other obiections taken from the difficulty of *Ainsworths* tunes, and the corruptions in

our

our common pſalme books, wee hope they are anſwered in this new edition of pſalmes which wee here preſent to God and his Churches. For although wee have cauſe to bleſſe God in many reſpects for the religious indeavours of the tranſlaters of the pſalmes into meetre uſually annexed to our Bibles, yet it is not unknowne to the godly learned that they have rather preſented a paraphraſe then the words of David tranſlated according to the rule 2 *chron.* 29. 30. and that their addition to the words, detractions from the words are not ſeldome and rare, but very frequent and many times needles, (which we ſuppoſe would not be approved of if the pſalmes were ſo tranſlated into proſe) and that their variations of the ſenſe, and alterations of the ſacred text too frequently, may iuſtly miniſter matter of offence to them that are able to com - pare the tranſlation with the text; of which failings, ſome iudicious have oft complained, others have been grieved, wherupon it hath bin generally deſired, that as wee doe inioye other, ſoe (if it were the Lords will) wee might inioye this ordinance alſo in its native purity: wee have therefore done our indeavour to make a plaine and familiar tranſlation of the pſalmes and words of David into engliſh metre, and have not ſoe much as preſumed to paraphraſe to give the ſenſe of his meaning in other words; we have therefore attended heerin as our chief guide the originall, ſhūning all additions, except ſuch as even the beſt tranſlators tranflators of them in profe fupply, avoiding all materiall dettactions from words or fence. The word יּ which wee tranflate *and* as it is redundant fometime in the Hebrew, foe fomtime (though not very often) it hath been left out, and yet not then, if the fence were not faire without it.

As for our tranflations, wee have with our englifh Bibles (to which next to the Originall wee have had refpect) ufed the Idioms of our owne tongue in ftead of Hebraifmes, left they might feeme englifh barbarifmes.

Synonimaes wee ufe indifferently: as *folk* for *people*, and *Lord* for *Iehovah*, and fomtime (though feldome) *God* for *Iehovah*; for which (as for fome other interpretations of places cited in the new Teftament) we have the fcriptures authority pf. 14. with 53. Heb. 1. 6. with pfalme 97. 7. Where a phrafe is doubtfull wee have followed that which (in our owne apprehenfiō) is moft genuine & edifying:

Somtime wee have contracted, fomtime dilated the fame hebrew word, both for the fence and the verfe fake: which dilatation wee conceive to be no paraphrafticall addition no more then the contraction of a true and full tranflation to be any unfaithfull detraction or diminution: as when wee dilate *who healeth* and fay *he it is who healeth*; foe when wee contract, *thofe that ftand in awe of God* and fay *Gods fearers*.

Laftly. Becaufe fome hebrew words have a

** 3   more

more full and emphaticall signification then any one english word can or doth somtime expresse, hence wee have done that somtime which faithfull tranflators may doe, *viz.* not only to tranflate the word but the emphasis of it; as אֵל *mighty God*, for *God*. בָּרַךְ *humbly bleffe* for *bleffe*; *rife to ftand*, pfalm 1. for *ftand*; *truth and faithfullnes* for *truth*. Howbeit, for the verfe fake wee doe not alway thus, yet wee render the word truly though not fully; as when wee fomtime fay *reioyce* for *fhout for ioye*.

As for all other changes of numbers, tenfes, and characters of fpeech, they are fuch as either the hebrew will unforcedly beare, or our englifh forceably calls for, or they no way change the fence; and fuch are printed ufually in an other character.

If therefore the verfes are not alwayes fo fmooth and elegant as fome may defire or expect; let them confider that Gods Altar needs not our pollifhings: Ex. 20. for wee have refpected rather a plaine tranflation, then to fmooth our verfes with the fweetnes of any paraphrafe, and foe have attended Confcience rather then Elegance, fidelity rather then poetry, in tranflating the hebrew words into englifh language, and Davids poetry into englifh meetre; that

Preface.

that foe wee may fing in Sion the Lords
fongs of prayfe according to his owne
will; untill hee take us from hence,
and wipe away all our teares , &
bid us enter into our mafters
ioye to fing eternall
Halleluiahs .

THE PSALMES

In Metre

PSALME I

O Blessed man, that in th'advice
  of wicked doeth not walk:
nor stand in sinners way, r or sit
  in chayre of scornfull folk.

2 But in the law of Iehovah,
  is his longing delight:
aud in his law doth meditate,
  by day and eke by night.

3 And he shall be like to a tree
  planted by water-rivers:
that in his season yeilds his fruit,
  and his leafe never withers.

4 And all he doth, shall prosper well,
  the wicked are not so:
but they are like vnto the chaffe,
  which winde drives to and fro.

5 Therefore shall not ungodly men,
  rise to stand in the doome,
nor shall the sinners with the just,
  in their assemblie come.

6 For of the righteous men, the Lord
  acknowledgeth the way:
but the way of vngodly men,
  shall vtterly decay.

A   PSALM

PSALM II

VVHy rage the *Heathen* furiously?
    muse vaine things people do;
2 Kings of the earth doe set themselves,
    Princes consult also:
    with one consent against the Lord,
    and his anoynted one.
3 Let us asunder break their bands,
    their cords bee from us throwne.
4 Who sits in heav'n shall laugh; the lord
    will mock them; then will he
5 Speak to them in his ire, and wrath:
    and vex them suddenlie.
6 But I annoynted have my King
    upon my holy hill
7 of Zion: The established
    counsell declare I will.
  God spake to me, thou art my Son:
    this day I thee begot.
8 Aske thou of me, and I will give
    the Heathen for thy lot:
    and of the earth thou shalt possesse
    the utmost coasts abroad.
9 thou shalt them break as Potters sherds
    and crush with yron rod.
10 And now yee Kings be wise, be learn'd
    yee Iudges of th'earth(*Heare.*)
11 Serve yee the lord with reverence,
    rejoyce in him with feare.
12 Kisse yee the Sonne, lest he be wroth,
    and yee fall in the way.
  when his wrath quickly burnes, oh blest⁵

are

are all that on him stay .

Psalme 3

1 A psalme of David when he fled from the
face of Absalom his Sonne.

O Lord, how many are my foes?
   how many up against me stand?

2 Many say to my soule noe helpe
   in God for him at any hand.

3 But thou Lord art my shield, my glory
   and the-uplifter of my head,

4 with voyce to God I cal'd, who from
   his holy hill me answered.

5 I layd me downe, I slept, I wakt,
   for Iehovah did me up beare:

6 People that set against me round,
   ten thousand of them I'le not feare.

7 Arise o Lord, save me my God,
   for all mine enimies thou hast stroke
   upon the cheek-bone :& the teeth
   of the ungodly thou hast broke.

8 This, and all such salvation,
   belongeth vnto Iehovah;
   thy blessing is, and let it be
   upon thine owne people. Selah.

Psalme 4

To the cheife Musician on *Neginoth*,
      a psalme of David.

GOD of my justice, when I call
   answer me: when distrest
thou hast inlarg'd me, shew me grace,
   and heare thou my request.

A 2   2 yee

2 Ye Sonnes of men, my glory turne
     to shame how long will you?
how long will ye love vanity,
     and still deceit pursue?
3 But know, the Lord doth for himselfe
     set by his gracious saint:
the Lord will heare when I to him
     doe poure out my complaint.
4 Be stirred up, but doe not sinne,
     consider seriouslie:
within your heart upon your bed,
     and wholly silent be
5 Let sacrifices of justice,
     for sacrifices be,
and confidently put your trust
     on Iehovah doe ye.
6 Many there be that say o who,
     will cause us good to see:
the light, Lord, of thy countenance
     let on us lifted be.
7 Thou hast put gladnesse in my heart,
     more then the time wherein
their corne, and also their new wine,
     have much increased bin.
8 In peace with him I will lye downe,
     and take my sleepe will I:
For thou Lord mak'st me dwell alone
     in confident safety.

Psalme 5

1 To the cheife Musitian upon *Nehiloth*,
     a psalme of David.

                                        psalm

PSALME V

Heare thou my words and underſtand
    my meditation, Iehovah.

2 My King, my God, attend the voyce
    of my cry: for to thee I pray.

3 At morn Iehovah, thou ſhalt heare
    my voyce: to thee I will addreſſe

4 at morn, I will looke up. For thou
    art not a God lov'ſt wickedneſſe
    neither ſhall evil with thee dwell.

5 Vaine glorious fooles before thine eyes
    ſhall never ſtand: for thou hateſt
    all them that worke iniquities.

6 Thou wilt bring to diſtruction
    the ſpeakers of lying-falſhood,
    the lord will make to be abhor'd
    the man deceitfull, and of blood.

7 But I will come into thine houſe
    in multitude of thy mercy:
    and will in feare of thee bow downe,
    in temple of thy ſanctity.

8 Lead me forth in thy rightouſnes,
    becauſe of mine obſerving ſpies,
    O Iehovah doe thou thy wayes
    make ſtraight, and plaine, before mine eyes

9 For there no truth is in his mouth,
    their inward part iniquities;
    their throat an open ſepulchre,
    their tongue is bent to flatteries.

10 O God make thou them deſolate
    from their owne plots let them fall far,
    caſt them out in their heapes of ſinnes,

for

for they against thee Rebells are.

11 And all that trust in thee shall joy,
and shout for joy eternallie,
and thou shalt them protect: & they
that love thy name shall joy in thee.

12 For thou Iehovah, wilt bestow
a blessing on the rightous one:
and wilt him crowne as with a sheild,
with gracious acceptation.

Psalme 6

To the chief Musician on *Neginoth* upon-
Sheminith, a psalme of David

LORD in thy wrath rebuke me not,
nor in thy hot wrath chasten me·

2 Pitty me Lord, for I am weak,
Lord heale me, for my bones vext be.

3 Also my soule is troubled sore:
how long Lord wilt thou me forsake?

4 Returne o Lord, my soule release:
o save me for thy mercy sake.

5 In death no mem'ry is of thee
and who shall prayse thee in the grave?

6 I faint with groanes, all night my bed
swims, I with tears my couch washt have.

7 mine eye with grief is dimme and old:
because of all mine enimies.

8 But now depart away fom me,
all yee that work iniquities:
for Iehovah ev'n now hath heard
the voyce of these my weeping teares.

9 Iehovah heare my humble suit,

Iehovah

Iehovah doth receive my prayers.

10 Let all mine enimies be asham'd
and greatly troubled let them be:
yea let them be returned back,
and be ashamed suddenlie.

Psalme 7

Shiggajon of David which he sãg to Iehovah
upõ the words of Cush the Benjamite.

O LORD my God in thee
I doe my trust repose,
save and deliver me from all
my persecuting foes.

2 Lest like a Lion hee
my soule in peeces teare:
rending asunder, while there is
not one deliverer.

3 Iehovah o my God
if this thing done have I :
if so there be within my hands
wrongfull iniquity

4 If I requited ill
the man with me at peace,
(yea I have him delivered
that was my foe causlesse:)

5 Let foe pursue my soule,
and take, and tread to clay
my life: and honor in the dust
there let him wholly lay

6 Arise Lord in thy wrath
for th'enimies fiercenesse:
be thou lift up, & wake to me,

A 4   judgemẽt

judgement thou did'st expresse.

7 So thee encompasse round
 shall peoples assembly;
and for the same doe thou returne,
 vnto the place on high.

8 The Lord shall judge the folke;
 Iehovah judge thou me.
according to my righteousnesse,
 and mine integritie.

9 Let ill mens malice cease,
 but doe the just confirme,
for thou who art the righteous God:
 dost hearts and reins discerne.

10 For God my sheild, the right
 in heart he saved hath.

11 The God that doth the rightous judge,
 yet daily kindleth wrath.

12 If he doe not returne,
 his sword he sharp will whet:
his bow he bended hath, and he
 the same hath ready set.

13 For him he hath prepar'd
 the instruments of death,
for them that hotly persecute,
 his arrows he sharpneth.

14 Behold he travelleth
 of vaine iniquity:
a toylesome mischeife he conceiv'd,
 but shall bring forth a lye.

15 A pit he digged hath,
 and delved deepe the same:

but

But fall'n he is into the ditch,
    that he himselfe did frame.
16 His mischeivous labour
    shall on his head turn downe:
and his injurious violence
    shall fall upon his crowne.
17 Iehovah I will prayse
    for his just equity;
and I will sing unto the name
    of Iehovah most high.

       Psalme 8
  To the chiefe Musician upon *Gittith*,
     a psalme of David.

O LORD our God in all the earth
    how's thy name wondrous great:
who hast thy glorious majesty
    above the heavens set.
2 out of the mouth of sucking babes.
    thy strength thou didst ordeine,
that thou mightst still the enemy,
    and them that thee disdaine.
3 when I thy fingers work, thy Heav'ns,
    the moone and starres consider
4 which thou hast set. What's wretched man
    that thou dost him remember?
or what's the Son of man, that thus
    him visited thou hast?
5 For next to Angells, thou hast him
    a litle lower plac't
and hast with glory crowned him,
    and comely majesty:

B

               6 and

6 And on thy works haſt given him,
    lordly authoriy.

7 All haſt thou put under his feet;
    all ſheep and oxen, yea

8 and beaſts of field. Foules of the ayre,
    and fiſhes of the ſea,
    and all that paſſe through paths of ſeas.

9 O Iehovah our Lord,
   how wondrouſly-magnificent
    is thy name through the world?

Pſalme 9

To the chiefe Muſician upon *Muth-Labben*
a pſalme of David

LORD I'le the prayſe, with all my heart;
   thy wonders all proclaime.

2 I will be glad and joy in thee;
   moſt high, I'le ſing thy name.

3 In turning back my foes, they'le fall
   and periſh at thy ſight.

4 For thou maintaines my right,& cauſe:
   In throne ſits judging right.

5 Thou t'heathen checkſt, & th'wicked ſtroyd;
   their names raz'd ever aye.

6 Thy ruines,foe, for aye are done;
   thou madſt their townes decaye;
  their memory with them is loſt.

7 Yet ever ſits the *L*ord:
  his throne to judgement he prepares.

8 With right he'l judge the world:
  he to the folke ſhall miniſter
   judgement in uprightneſſe.

9 The

9 The Lord is for th'oprest a'fort:
    a fort in times of ftreffe.
10 Who knowes thy name, will truft in thce;
    nor doft thou, Lord forfake,
11 them that thee feek. Pfalmes, to the Lord
    that dwells in Sion, make:
  declare among the folk his works.
12 For blood when he doth feeke,
 he them remembers: nor forgets
    the crying of the meeke.

        (2)

13 Iehovah, mercy on me have,
    from them that doe me hate
 marke mine afflictions that arife,
    thou lift'ft me from deaths-gate.
14 That I may tell in the gates of
    the Daughter of Sion,
 thy prayfes all: and may rejoyce
    in thy falvation.
15 The heathen are funk downe into
    the pit that they had made:
 their owne foot taken is ith'net
    which privily they layd.
16 By judgement which he executes
    Iehovah is made knowne:
 the wicked's fnar'd in's owne hand work.
    deepe meditation.
17 The wicked fhall be turn'd to hell,
    all lands that God forget.
18 Forgot the needy fhall ne're be:
  poores hope ne're faild him yet.

19 Arise, o Lord, lest men prevaile,
      judge t'heathen in thy sight.

20 That they may know they be but men,
      the nations Lord affright.   Selah

Psalme 10

WHy standst thou Lord a far? why hyd'st
      thy selfe in times of streight?

2 In pride the wicked persecutes
      the poore afflicted wight:
   snare them in their contrived plots.

3   For of his hearts desire
   the wicked boasts, and covetous
      blesseth, stirring Gods ire.

4 The wicked one by reason of
      his countenances pride
   will not seek *after God*: not God
      so all his thoughts abide.

5 his wayes doe alwayes bring forth griefe,
      on high thy judgements bee
   above his sight: his pressing foes
      puffe at them all will hee.

6 Within his heart he thus hath sayd,
      I moved shall not bee:
   from aye to aye because I *am*
      not in adversitie.

7 His mouth with cursing filled *is*,
      deceits, and fallacy:
   under his tongue perversnes *is*,
      also iniquity.

8 In the close places of the townes
      he sits, in secret dens

                                          he

he slays the harmlesse: 'gainst the poore
slyly his eyes downe bends.

9 He closely lurks as lion lurks
in den, the poore to catch
he lurks, & trapping them in 's net
th' afflicted poore doth snatch.

10 Downe doth he crowtch,& to the dust
humbly he bowes *with-all*:
that so a multitude of poore
in his strong pawes may fall .

11 He saith in heart, God hath forgot:
he hides his face away,
so that he will not see this thing
unto eternall aye.

(2)

12 Iehovah rise thou up,o God
lift thou thine hand on hy,
let not the meek afflicted one
be out of memory.

13 Wherefore doth the ungodly man
contemne th' almighty one?
he in his heart saith, thou wilt not
make inquisition.

14 Thou seest,for thou markst wrong,& spight,
with thy hand to repay:
the poore leavs it to thee,thou art
of fatherlesse the stay.

15 Break thou the arme of the wicked,
and of the evil one.
search thou out his impiety,
untill thou findest none.

B 3   16 Iehov-

16 Iehovah king for ever is,
    and to eternall aye:
out of his land the heathen folke
    are perished away.

17 The meeke afflicted-mans desire
    Iehovah,thou dost heare:
thou firmly dost prepare their heart,
    thou makst attent thine eare.

18 To judge the fatherlesse & poore:
    that adde no more he may
sorrowfull man out of the land
    with terror to dismay.

Psalme 11

To the chiefe Musician a psalme
of David.

I In the Lord do trust,how then
    to my soule doe ye say,
as doth a litle bird unto
    your mountaine flye away?

2 For loe, the wicked bend their bow,
    their arrows they prepare
on string;to shoot in dark at them
    in heart that upright are.

3 If that the firme foundationes,
    utterly ruin'd bee:
as for the man that righteous is,
    what then performe can hee?

4 The Lord in's holy temple is,
    the Lords throne in heaven:
his eyes will view, and his eye lids
    will prove the Sonnes of men.

5 The man that truly-righteous *is*
    ev'n him the Lord will prove;
his soule the wicked hates,& him
    that violence doth love.

6 Snares,fire, & brimstone he will raine,
    ungodly men upon:
and burning tempest;of their cup
    shall-be their portion.

7 For Iehovah that righteous is,
    all righteousnesse doth love:
his countenane the upright one
    beholding, doth approve.

Psalme 12

To the chiefe Musician upon *Sheminith*
a psalme of David.

HElpe Lord: for godly men doe cease:
    faithfull faile men among.

2 Each to his freind speaks vanity;
    with flattring lips, *and tongue*
and with a double heart they speake.

3 All flatt'ring lips the Lord
shall cut them of,with every tongue
    that speaketh boasting word.

4 Thus have they sayd,we with our tongue,
    prevailing pow're shall get :
are not our lips our owne.for Lord
    who over us is set?

5 Thus saith the Lord, for sighs of them
    that want,for poor opprest,
I 'le now arise,from such as puffe,
    will set him safe at rest.

B 4   6 pure

6 Pure are the words the Lord doth speak:
   as silver that is tryde
   in earthen furnace, seven times
   that hath been purifyde.

7 Thou shalt them keep, o Lord, thou shalt
   preserve them ev'ry one,
   For evermore in safety from
   this generation.

8 The wicked men on evry side
   doe walk presumptuously,
   when as the vilest sons of men
   exalted are on hye.

Psalme 13

To the chiefe Musician: a psalme
of David.

O IEHOVAH, how long
   wilt thou forget me aye?
how long wilt thou thy countenance
   hide from me farre away?

2 How long shall I counsell,
   in my soule take, sorrow
   in my heart dayly? o're me set
   how long shall be my foe?

3 Iehovah, o my God,
   behold me answer make,
   Illuminate mine eyes, lest I
   the sleepe of death doe take.

4 Lest my foe say, I have
   prevaild 'gainst him: & me
those who doe trouble, doe rejoyce,
   when I shall moved bee.

5 But

5 But I asured trust
    have put in thy mercy;
my heart in thy salvation
    shall joy exceedingly.
6 Vnto Iehovah I
    will sing, because that hee,
for evil bountifully hath
    rewarded good to mee.

Psalme 14

To the chiefe Musician a psalme of Dauid.

THe foole in's heart saith ther's no God;
    they are corrupt, have done
abominable-practises,
    that doth good there is none.
2 The Lord from heaven looked downe
    on Sonnes of men: to see,
if any that doth understand,
    that seeketh God there bee.
3 All are gone back, together they
    ev'n filthy are become:
and there is none that doeth good,
    noe not so much as one.
4 The workers of iniquityes,
    have they no knowledge all?
that eate my people: they eate bread,
    and on God doe not call.
5 There with a very grievous feare
    affrighted sore they were,
for God in generation is
    of such as righteous are.

C   ● the

6 The counsell yee would make of him
    that poore afflicted is,
to be asham'd & that because
    the Lord his refuge is.

7 Who Israels health from Syon gives?
    his folks captivitie
when God shall turne: Iacob shall joye
    glad Israel shall be.

Psalme 15
A psalme of David.

IEHOVAH, who shall in thy tent
    so ourne, and who is hee
shall dwell within thy holy mount?

2 He that walks uprightlie,
    And worketh justice, and speaks truth

3 in s heart, And with his tongue
he doth not slander, neither doth
    unto his neighbour wrong,
And 'gainst his neighbour that doth not
    take up reproachfull lyes.

4 Hee that an abject person is
    contemn'd is in his eyes;
But he will highly honour them
    that doe Iehovah feare:
and changeth not, though to his losse,
    if that he once doe sweare.

5 Nor gives his coyne to usury,
    and bribe he doth not take
against the harmelesse. he that doth
    these things shall never shake.

Pfalme 16

Michtam of David

O Mighty God, preſerve thou mee,
for on thee dœ I reſt.

2 Thou art my God, vnto the Lord
my ſoule thou haſt profeſt:
My goodnes reacheth not to thee.

3 But to the Saints upon
the earth & to the excellent,
whome all my joye is on.

4 They who give gifts to a ſtrange God,
their ſorrowes multiplye:
their drink oblations of blood
offer up will not I.
Neither will I into my lips
the names of them take up.

5 Iehovah is the portion
of my part, & my cup:
Thou art maintainer of my lot.

6 To me the lines fal'n bee
in pleaſant places: yea, faire is
the heritage for mee.

7 I will Iehovah humbly-bleſſe,
who hath mee counſelled:
yea in the nights my reines have mee,
chaſtiſing nurtured.

8 Iehovah I have alwayes ſet
as preſent before mee:
becauſe he is at my right hand
I ſhall not moved bee.

9 Wherefore my heart rejoyced hath,

C 2

and

and glad is my glory:
moreover also my flesh shall
in hope lodge securely.
10 Because thou wilt not leave my soule
within the grave to bee,
nor wilt thou give thine holy one,
corruption for to see.
11 Thou wilt shew me the path of life,
of joyes abundant-store
before thy face, at thy right hand
are pleasures evermore.

Psalme 17
A Prayer of David.

HArken, o Lord, unto the right,
  attend vnto my crye,
give eare vnto my pray'r, that goes
from lips that doe not lye.
2 From thy face let my judgement come:
thine eyes the right let see.
3 Thou provst mine heart, thou visitest
by night, and tryest mee.
yet nothing find'st, I have resolvd
my mouth shall not offend.
4 From mens works: by word of thy lips
I spoylers paths attend.
5 Stay my feet in thy paths, lest my
6 steps slip. I cal'd on thee,
for thou wilt heare, God, heare my speech,
incline thine eare to mee.
7 O thou that sav'st by thy right hand,
thy merveilous-mercyes,

shew

ſhew vnto them that truſt in thee,
 from ſuch as 'gainſt them riſe.
(2)

8 As apple of thine eye mee keepe.
 In thy wings ſhade mee hide.
9 From wicked who mee waſt : my foes
 in heart are on each ſide.
10 Cloſ'd in their fat they are: & they
 ſpeak with their mouth proudly.
11 They round us in our ſtepps: they ſeſ
 on earth their bow'd downe eye.
12 His likenes as a lion is,
 that greedy is to teare,
in ſecret places lurking as
 hee a young lion were.
13 Him, in his ſight, riſe, diſappoynt
 make him bow downe o Lord,
doe thou my ſoule deliver from
 the wicked one, thy ſword,
14 From mortall men thine hand, o Lord
 from men that mortall are,
and of this paſſing-world, who have
 within this life their ſhare,
with thy hid treaſure furthermore
 whoſe belly thou filleſt:
their ſonnes are fil'd, & to their babes
 of wealth they leave the reſt.
15 In righteouſnes, thy favour I
 ſhall very clearely ſee,
and waking with thine image, I
 ſhall ſatiſſied bee.

C 3

Pſalme 18

To the chiefe Muſician, a *pſalme* of Dauid, the ſervant of
the Lord, who ſpake the words of this Song, in the day that
the Lord deliuered him from the hands of all his enemies,
& from the hand of Saule, and hee Sayde,

I'Le dearely love thee, Lord, my ſtrength.
  The Lord is my rock, and my towre
  and my deliverer, my God,
  I'le truſt in him *who is* my powre,
  My ſhield, & my ſalvationes-horne,

3 my high-fort; Who is prayſe worthy:
  I on the Lord will call, ſo ſhall
  I bee kept from mine enemye.

4 Deaths ſorrowes mee encompaſſed,
  mee fear'd the floods of ungodlie,

5 Hells pangs beſet me round abour,
  the ſnares of death prevented mee.

6 I in my ſtreights, cal'd on the Lord,
  and to my God cry'd: he did heare
  from his temple my voyce, my crye,
  before him came, unto his eare.

7 Then th' earth ſhooke, & quak'r, & moūtaines
  roots moov'd, & were ſtird at his ire,

8 Vp from his noſtrils went a ſmoak,
  and from his mouth devouring fire:
  By it the coales inkindled were.

9 Likewiſe the heavens he dowre-bow'd,
  and he deſcended, & there was
  under his feet a gloomy cloud.

10 And he on cherub rode, and flew;
  yea he flew on the wings of winde.

11 His ſecret place hee darknes made

his

his covert that him round confinde,
Dark waters, & thick clouds of skies.

12 From brightnes,that before him was,
his thickned clouds did passe away,
hayl-stones and coales of fire did passe.

13 Also Iehovah thundered,
within the heavens,the most high
likewise his angry-voyce did give,
hayl-stones, and coales of fire *did fly.*

14 Yea he did out his arrows send,
and bruising he them scattered,
and lightnings hee did multiply,
likewise he them discomfited.

15 The waters channels then were seene,
and the foundationes of the world
appear'd,at thy rebuke,at blast,
of the breath of thy nostrils Lord.

(2)

16 Hee from above sent hee me took:
me out of waters-great he drew.

17 Hee from mine enemies-strong, & from
them which me hated did rescue:
For they were mightyer then I.

18 They mee prevented in the day
of my cloudy calamity;
but for me was the Lord a stay.

19 And hee me to large place brought forth:
hee sav'd mee, for he did delight

20 in mee. The Lord rewarded me
according as I did aright,
According to the cleannesse of

my

my hands, he recompenced mee.

21 For the wayes of the Lord I kept:
nor from my God went wickedlie.

22 For all his judgements mee before:
nor from me put I his decree.

23 With him I upright was, and kept
my selfe from mine iniquitie.

24 The Lord hath recompenced mee,
after my righteousnes therefore:
according to the cleannesse of
my hands that was his eyes before.

25 With mercifull, thou mercifull,
with upright thou deales uprightly.

26 With pure thou pure, thou also wilt
with froward turne thy selfe awry.

27 For thou wilt save th'afflicted folke:
but wilt the lofty looks suppresse.

28 For thou wilt light my lampe: the Lord,
my God will lighten my darknesse.

29 For by the I rann through a troupe,
and by my God leapt o're a wall.

30 Gods way is perfect: Gods word tryde:
that trust in him hee's shield to all.

31 For who is God except the Lord?
or who a rock, our God except?

32 Its God that girdeth me with strength,
and hee doth make my way perfect.

33 Like to the hyndes he makes my feet:
and on my high place maks me stand.

34 Mine armes doe break a bow of brasse;
so well to warre he learnes my hand.

35 The shield of thy salvation
    thou furthermore hast given mee:
    and thy right-hand hath mee upheld,
    thy meeknes made mee great to bee.

36 Vnder mee thou makst large my steps,
    so that mine anckles did not slyde

37 My foes pursu'de I, & them caught:
    nor turn'd I till they were destroyd.

38 I wounded them & they could not
    rise up: under my feet they fell.

39 Because that thou hast girded mee
    with fortitude to the battel:
    Thou hast subdued under mee,
    those that did up against me rise.

40 And my foes necks thou gavest mee,
    that I might wast mine enemyes.

41 They cryde but there was none to save,
    to God, yet with no answer meet.

42 I beat them then as dust i'th winde
    and cast them out as dirt i'th street.

(4)

43 And thou from the contentions
    hast of the people mee set free;
    thou of the heathen mad'st me head:
    people I knew not shall serve mee.

44 They'le at first hearing me obey:
    strangers shall yield themselvs to mee.

45 The strangers shall consume away,
    and from their closets frighted bee.

46 The Lord lives, and blest be my Rock,
    let my healths God exalted bee.

D   47 Its

47 It's God for mee that vengeance works,
  and brings downe people under mee .

48 Mee from mine enemies he doth save:
  and above those that 'gainst me went,
  thou lift'st me up; and thou hast freed
  mee from the man that's violent.

49 I with confession will therefore
  unto thee render thanksgiving,
  o Lord, among the heathen-folk;
  and to thy name I'le prayses sing:

50 He giveth great deliverance
  to his King, and doth shew mercy
  to his annoynted, to David,
  and to his seed eternally.

Psalme 19

To the chiefe musician a psalme of David.

THe heavens doe declare
    the majesty of God:
  also the firmament shews forth
    his handy-work abroad.

2 Day speaks to day, knowledge
    night hath to night declar'd.

3 There neither speach nor language is,
    where their voyce is not heard.

4 Through all the earth their line
    is gone forth, & unto
  the utmost end of all the world,
    their speaches reach also:
  A Tabernacle hee
    in them pitcht for the Sun.

5 Who Bridegroom like from's chamber goes
                                    glad

glad Giants-race to run.
6 From heavens utmost end,
  his course and compassing,
to ends of it, & from the heat
  thereof is hid nothing.

(2)

7 The Lords law perfect is,
  the soule converting back:
Gods testimony faithfull is,
  makes wise who-wisdome-lack.
8 The statutes of the Lord,
  are right, & glad the heart:
the Lords commandement is pure,
  light doth to eyes impart.
9 Iehovahs feare is cleane,
  and doth indure for ever:
the judgements of the Lord are true,
  and righteous altogether.
10 Then gold, then much fine gold,
  more to be prized are,
then hony, & the hony-comb,
  sweeter they are by farre.
11 Also thy servant is
  admonished from hence:
and in the keeping of the same
  is a full recompence.
12 Who can his errors know?
  from secret faults cleanse mee.
13 And from presumptuous-sins, let thou
  kept back thy servant bee:
Let them not beare the rule

D 2

in me, & then shall I
be perfect, and shall cleansed bee
from much iniquity.

14 Let the words of my mouth,
and the thoughts of my heart,
be pleasing with thee, Lord, my Rock
who my redeemer art.

Psalme 20

To the chiefe Musician, a psalme of David.

IEHOVAH heare thee in the day
of sore calamity,
the name of the God of Iacob
defend thee mightily.

2 Send thee help from his holy place,
from Sion strengthen thee.

3 Minde all thy gifts, thy sacrifice
accepted let it bee.   Selah.

4 Grant thee according to thy heart,
all thy counsell fulfill.

5 In thy perfect salvation
with singing joy we will:
And we in the name of our God
our banners will erect:
when as all thy petitions
Iehovah shall effect.

6 Now I know, that Iehovah doth
save his annoynted-Deare:
with saving strength of his right hand
from his pure heav'n will heare.

7 In charrets some their confidence,
and some in horses set:

but

but we the name of Iehovah
   our **God** will not forget.

8 They are brought downe & fal'n: but we,
   rise and stand stedfastly.

9 Save *Lord*,& let the King us heare
   when as to him we cry.

Psalme 21

To the chiefe Musician a psalme
of David.

IEHOVAH, in thy strength
   the King shall joyfull bee;
and joy in thy salvation
   how vehemently shall hee?

2 Thou of his heart to him
   hast granted the desire:
and thou hast not witholden back,
   what his lips did require.   Selah.

3 For thou dost with blessings
   of goodnes prevent him:
thou on his head of finest gold
   hast set a Diadem.

4 Of thee hee asked life,
   to him thou gav'st it free,
even length of days for evermore
   unto eternitie.

5 In thy salvation
   his glory hath bene great:
honour, and comely dignity
   thou hast upon him set.

6 For thou him blessings setst
   to perpetuitie:

Thou makſt him with thy countenance
    exceeding glad to bee.
7 Becauſe that in the Lord
    the King doth truſt, & hee
through mercy of the higheſt one,
    ſhall not removed bee.
8 The Lord ſhall finde out all
    that are thine enemies:
thy right hand alſo ſhall finde out
    thoſe that doe thee deſpiſe.
9 Thou ſetſt as fiery oven
    them in times of thine ire:
the Lord will ſwallow them in's wrath
    and them conſume with fire.
10 Thou wilt deſtroy the fruit,
    that doth proceed of them,
out of the earth: & their ſeed from
    among the Sonnes of men.
11 Becauſe they evill have
    intended againſt thee:
a wicked plot they have deviſ'd,
    but ſhall not able bee.
12 For thou wilt as a butt
    them ſet; & thou wilt place
thine arrows ready on thy ſtring,
    full right againſt their face.
13 Lord, in thy fortitude
    exalted bee on high:
and wee will ſing; yea prayſe with pſalmes
    thy mighty powr will wee.

Psalme 22
To the chiefe musician upon *Aijeleth Shahar*
a psalme of David.

MY God, my God, wherefore hast thou
forsaken mee? & why,
art thou so farre from helping mee,
from the words of my cry?

2 O my God, I doe cry by day,
but mee thou dost not heare;
and eke by night, & unto mee
no quiet rest is there.

3 Neverthelesse thou holy art,
who constantly dost dwell,
within the thankfull prayses of
thy people Israell.

4 Our fore-fathers in thee have put
assured confidence:
they trusted have, & thou to them
didst give deliverance.

5 Vnto thee they did cry aloud,
and were delivered:
in thee they put their confidence,
and were not confounded.

6 But I a worme, & not a man;
of men an opprobrie,
and also of the people am
despis'd contempruouslie.

7 All they that doe upon mee look,
a scoffe at mee doe make:
they with the lip doe make a mow,
the head in scorne they shake.

upõ

8 Vpon the Lord he rold himselfe,
  let him now rid him quite:
let him deliver him, becaufe
  in him he doth delight.

9 But thou art hee that me out of
  the belly forth didft take:
when I was on my mothers breafts,
  to hope thou didft mee make.

10 Vnto thee from the tender-womb
  committed been have I:
yea thou haft been my mighty-God
  from my mothers belly.

(2)

11 Be thou not farre away ftom mee,
  for tribulation
exceeding great is neere at hand,
  for helper there is none.

12 Mee many buls on every fide
  about have compaffed:
the mighty- buls of Bafhan have
  mee round invironed.

13 They have with their wide-opened-mouths
  fo gaped mee upon;
like as it were a ravening
  and a roaring Lion.

14 As water I am poured-our,
  and all my bones fundred:
my heart in midft of my bowels,
  is like to wax melted.

15 My ftrength like a potfherd is dryde;
  and my tongue faft cleaveth

           unto

unto my jawes,& thou haſt brought
   me to the duſt of death.

16 For dogs have compaſt me abour;
   thᶜ aſſembly me beſet
  of the wicked; they pierced through
   my hands, alſo my feet.

17 My bones I may them number all:
   they lookt, they did me view.

18 My cloths among them they did part:
   and lot for my coat threw.

19 But thou Lord be not far, my ſtrength,
   to help me haſten thou.

20 My ſoule from ſword, my darling from
   the powre of dogs reſcue.

21 And from the mouth of the Lion
   give me ſalvation free:
  for thou from hornes of Vnicornes
   anſwer haſt given mee.

22 Thy name, I will declare to them
   that Brethren are to mee:
  in midſt of congregation
   I will give prayſe to thee.

(3)

23 Yee that doe feare the Lord prayſe him,
   all Iacobs ſeed prayſe yee,
  him glorify,& dread him all
   yee Iſraels ſeed that bee.

24 For he the poors affliction
   loaths not, nor doth deſpiſe;
  nor hides his face from him, but heats
   when unto him hee cryes.

E   25 concern-

25 Concerning thee shall be my prayse
in the great assembly:
before them that him reverence
performe my vowes will I.

25 The meek shall eat & be suffic'd:
Iehovah prayse shall they
that doe him seek: your heart shall live
unto perpetuall aye.

27 All ends of th'earth remember shall
and turne unto the Lord:
and thee all heathen-families
to worship shall *accord*.

28 Because unto Iehovah doth
the kingdome appertaine:
and he among the nations
is ruler Soveraigne.

29 Earths-fat-ones, eat & worship shall:
all who to dust descend,
(though none can make alive his soule)
before his face shall bend.

30 With service a posterity
him shall attend upon;
to God it shall accounted bee
a generation.

31 Come shall they, & his righteousnes
by them declar'd shall bee,
unto a people yet unborne,
that done this thing hath hee.

23   *A Psalme of David.*

THe Lord to mee a shepheard is,
want therefore shall not I.

2 Hee

2 Hee in the folds of tender-graſſe,
  doth cauſe mee downe to lie:
  To waters calme me gently leads
3 Reſtore my ſoule doth hee:
  he doth in paths of righteouſnes:
  for his names ſake leade mee.
4 Yea though in valley of deaths ſhade
  I walk, none ill I'le feare:
  becauſe thou art with mee, thy rod,
  and ſtaffe my comfort are.
5 For mee a table thou haſt ſpread,
  in preſence of my foes:
  thou doſt annoynt my head with oyle,
  my cup it over-flowes.
6 Goodnes & mercy ſurely ſhall
  all my dayes follow mee:
  and in the Lords houſe I ſhall dwell
  ſo long as dayes ſhall bee.

Pſalme 24

A pſalme of david.

THe earth Iehovahs is,
  and the fulneſſe of it:
  the habitable world, & they
  that there upon doe ſit.
2 Becauſe upon the ſeas,
  hee hath it firmly layd:
  and it upon the water-floods
  moſt ſollidly hath ſtayd.
3 The mountaine of the Lord,
  who ſhall thereto aſcend?
  and in his place of holynes,

E 2

who

who is it that shall stand?
4 The cleane in hands, & pure
in heart;to vanity
who hath not lifted up his soule,
nor sworne deceitfully.

5 From God he shall receive
a benediction,
and righteousnes from the strong-God
of his salvation.

6 This is the progenie
of them that seek thy face:
of them that doe inquire for him:
of Iacob 'tis the race.   Selah.

7 Yee gates lift-up your heads,
and doors everlasting,
be yee lift up: & there into
shall come the glorious-King.

8 Who is this glorious King?
Iehovah, puissant,
and valiant, Iehovah is
in battel valiant.

9 Yee gates lift-up your heads,
and doors everlasting,
doe yee lift-up: & there into
shall come the glorious-King.

10 Who is this glorious-King?
loe, it is Iehovah
of warlike armies, hee the King
of glory is; Selah.

Psalme 25
A psalme of David.

PSALM

PSALME XXV.

I Lift my soule to thee o Lord.
My God I trust in thee,
let mee not be asham'd: nor let
my foes joy over mee.

3 Yea, all that wait on thee shall not,
be fill'd with shamefulnes:
but they shall be ashamed all,
who without cause transgresse.

4 Thy wayes, Iehovah, make mee know,
thy paths make me discerne.

5 Cause mee my steps to order well,
in thy truth, & mee learne,
For thou God of my saving health,
on thee I wait all day.

6 Thy bowels, Lord, & thy mercyes
minde; for they are for aye.

7 Sinnes of my youth remember not,
neither my trespasses:
after thy mercy minde thou mee
o Lord for thy goodnes.

8 Good and upright God is, therefore
will sinners teach the way.

9 The meek he'le guide in judgement: &
will teach the meek his way.

10 Iehovahs paths they mercy are,
all of them truth also;
to them that keep his covenant,
and testimonies do.

(2)

11 For thy names sake o Iehovah,
freely doe thou remitt

E 3   mine

mine owne perverse iniquitie:
   because that great is it.

12 Who fears the Lord, him hee will teach
   the way that he shall chuse.

13 his soule shall dwell at ease, his seed
   as heirs the earth shall vse.

14 The secret of God is with those
   that doe him reverence:
and of his covenant he them
   will give intelligence.

15 Mine eyes continually are
   upon Iehovah set:
for it is hee that will bring forth
   my feet out of the net.

16 Vnto me-wards turne thou thy face,
   and on mee mercy show:
because I solitary am
   afflicted poore also.

17 My hearts troubles inlarged are;
   from my distresse me bring.

18 See mine affliction,& my paine;
   and pardon all my sin.

19 Mark my foes; for they many are,
   and cruelly mee hate,

20 My soule keep,free mee;nor let mee
   be sham'd,who on thee wait.

21 Let soundnes,& uprightnesse keep
   mee: for I trust in thee.

22 Israel from his troubles all,
   o God, doe thou set free.

     25 *A psalme* of david.

I Vdge mee, o Lord, for I have walkt
  in mine integrity:
   and I have trusted in the Lord,
    therefore slyde shall not I.

2 Examine mee, Lord, & mee prove;
   my reins, & my heart try.

3 For thy grace is before mine eyes;
   and in thy truth walk I.

4 I sat not with vaine men, nor goe
   with men themselves that hide.

5 Evill mens company I hate:
   nor will with vile abide.

6 In cleannesse, Lord, I'le wash mine hands,
   so I'le thine altar round:

7 That I may preach with thankfull-voyce,
   and all thy prayses sound.

8 The habitation of thy house,
   Lord, dearly love doe I,
  the place and tabernacle of
   thy glorious majesty.

9 My soule with sinners gather not,
   with men of blood my life.

10 In whose hand 's guile, in whose right hand
   bribery is full rife.

11 Redeeme, & pitty mee; for I'le
   walk in mine uprightnesse.

12 My foot stands right: in th'assembly
   I will Iehovah blesse.

    27 *A* Psalme of David.

T He Lord my light, & my health is,
  what shall make me dismaid?

the

PSALM XXVII.

The Lord is my lifes-strength, of whom
    should I *then* be afrayd?
2 When wicked men, mine enemies,
    and my foes in battel;
    against mee come, to eate my flesh,
    themselves stumbled & fell.

3 If that an hoast against mee camp,
    my heart undaunted is:
    if war against mee should arise,
    I am secure in this.

4 One thing of God I asked have,
    which I will still request:
    that I may in the house of God,
    all dayes of my life rest:
    To see the beauty of the Lord,
    and in his Temple seeke.

5 For in his tent in th'evill-day,
    hidden hee will mee keepe:
    Hee will me hide in secrecy
    of his pavillion:
    and will me highly lift upon
    the rocks-munition.

6 Moreover at this-time my head
    lifted on high shall bee,
    above mine enemies, who doe
    about encompasse mee.
    Therefore in's tent I'le sacrifice,
    of joye an offering,
    unto Iehovah, sing will I,
    yea, I will prayses sing.

(2)

7 When as I with my voyce doe cry,
    mee, o Iehovah, heare;
have mercy also upon mee,
    and unto mee answer.

8 *When thou didst say*, seek yee my face,
    my heart sayd unto thee,
thy countenance, o Iehovah,
    it shall be sought by mee.

9 Hide not thy face from mee, nor off
    in wrath thy servant cast:
God of my health, leave, leave not mee,
    my helper been thou hast.

10 My father & my mother both
    though they doe mee forsake,
yet will Iehovah gathering
    unto himselfe me take.

11 Iehovah, teach thou mee the way,
    and be a guide to mee
in righteous path, because of them
    that mine observers bee.

12 Give mee not up unto the will
    of my streight-enemies:
for witnesse false against me stand,
    and breath out cruelties.

13 *I should haue fainted*, had not I
    believed for to see,
Iehovahs goodnes in the land
    of them that living bee.

14 Doe thou upon Iehovah waite:
    bee stablished, & let

F

thine

thine heart be strengthened,& thine hope
upon Iehovah set.
Psalme 28.
A psalme of David.

IEHOVAH,unto thee I cry,
 my Rock,be thou not deafe me fro:
lest thou be dumb from mee & I
be like them downe to pit that go.

2 Heare thou the voyce of my request
for grace, when unto thee I cry:
when I lift up mine hands unto
thine Oracle of Sanctity.

3 With ill men draw me not away,
with workers of unrighteousnes,
that with their neighbours peace doe speak,
but in their hands is wickednes.

4 Give thou to them like to their works
and like the evill of their deeds:
give them like to their handy-works,
and render unto them their meeds.

5 Because unto Iehovahs work
they did not wise-attention yeild,
neither unto his handy work,
them he will wast,but not up-build.

6 The Lord be blest, for he hath heard
the voyce of my requests for grace.

7 God is my strength,my shield,in him
my heart did trust, & helpt I was:
Therefore my heart will gladnes shew,
and with my song I'le him confesse.

8 The Lord of his annoynted ones

         their

their ftrength, & towre of fafety is.
9 Salvation to thy people give,
    and bleffe thou thine inheritance,
    and ev'n unto eternity
    doe thou them feed & them advance.

This. After the common tunes.

Save *Lord*, thy people, & doe thou
    bleffe thine inheritance:
and unto all eternity
    them feed & them advance.

Pfalme 29
A pfalme of David.
VNto the Lord doe yee afcribe
    (o Sonnes of the mighty)
unto the Lord doe yee afcribe
    glory & potency.
2 Vnto the Lord doe yee afcribe
    his names glorious renowne,
in beauty of his holynes
    unto the Lord bow downe.
3 The mighty voyce of Iehovah
    upon the waters is:
the God of glory thundereth,
    God on great waters is.
4 Iehovahs voyce is powerfull,
    Gods voyce is glorious,
5 Gods voyce breaks Cedars:yea God breaks
    Cedars of Lebanus.
6 He makes them like a calfe to fkip:

F 2

the

the mountaine Lebanon,
and like to a young Vnicorne
the hill of Syrion.

7 Gods voyce divides the flames of fire.

8 Iehovahs voyce doth make
the defart fhake: the Lord doth caufe
the Cadefh-defart fhake.

9 The Lords voyce makes the hindes to calve,
and makes the forreft bare:
and in his temple every one
his glory doth declare.

10 The Lord fate on the flouds: the Lord
for ever fits as King.

11 God to his folk gives ftrength: the Lord
his folk with peace blefling.

Pfalme 30
A Pfalme & Song, *at* the dedication
of the houfe of David.

IEHOVAH, I will thee extoll,
for thou haft lift up mee;
and over mee thou haft not made
my foes joyfull to bee.

2 O Lord my God, to thee I cry'de
and thou haft made mee whole.

3 Out of the grave, o Iehovah,
thou haft brought up my foule:
Thou mad'ft mee live, I went not downe

4 to pit. Sing to the Lord,
(yee his Saints) & give thanks when yee
his holynes record.

5 For but a moment in his wrath;

life

life in his love doth stay:
weeping may lodge with us a night
but joye at break of day.

6 I sayd in my prosperity,
    I shall be moved never.

7 Lord by thy favour thou hast made
    my mountaine stand fast ever:
  Thou hidst thy face,I troubled was.

8 I unto thee did cry,
  o Lord: also my humble suit
  unto the Lord made I.

9 What gaine is in my blood; when I
    into the pit goe downe?
  shall dust give glory unto thee?
  shall it thy truth make knowne?

10 Doe thou mee o Iehovah,heare,
    and on mee mercy have:
  Iehovah,o bee thou to mee
    an helper me to save.

11 Thou into dancing for my sake
    converted hast my sadnes:
  my sackcloth thou unloosed hast,
    and girded me with gladnes:

12 That sing to thee my glory may,
    and may not silent bee:
  o Lord my God,I will give thanks
    for evermore to thee.

Psalme 31
To the chief Musician, a psalme
of David.

PSALM

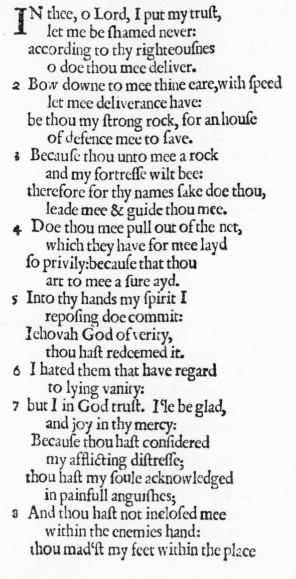

IN thee, o Lord, I put my trust,
    let me be shamed never:
according to thy righteousnes
    o doe thou mee deliver.

2 Bow downe to mee thine eare,with speed
    let mee deliverance have:
be thou my strong rock, for an house
    of defence mee to save.

3 Because thou unto mee a rock
    and my fortresse wilt bee:
therefore for thy names sake doe thou,
    leade mee & guide thou mee.

4 Doe thou mee pull out of the net,
    which they have for mee layd
so privily:because that thou
    art to mee a sure ayd.

5 Into thy hands my spirit I
    reposing doe commit:
Iehovah God of verity,
    thou hast redcemed it.

6 I hated them that have regard
    to lying vanity:

7 but I in God trust. I'le be glad,
    and joy in thy mercy:
Because thou hast considered
    my afflicting distresse;
thou hast my soule acknowledged
    in painfull anguishes;

8 And thou hast not inclosed mee
    within the enemies hand:
thou mad'st my feet within the place

of liberty to stand.

(2)

9 Have mercy upon mee, o Lord,
    for in distresse am I,
  with grief mine eye consumed is,
    my soule & my belly.

10 For my life with grief & my years
    with sighs are consumed:
  because of my sin, my strength failes,
    and my bones are wasted.

11 To all my foes I was a scorne,
    chiefly my neighbours to;
  a feare to freinds: they that saw mee
    without, did flye me fro.

12 I am forgot as a dead man
    that's out of memory:
  and like a vessel that is broke
    ev'n such a one am I.

13 Because that I of many men
    the slandering did heare,
  round about me on every side
    there was exceeding feare:
  While as that they did against mee
    counsell together take,
  they craftily have purposed
    my life away to make.

14 But o Iehovah, I in thee
    my confidence have put

15 I sayd thou art my God. My times
    within thy hand *are shut*:
  From the hands of mine enemies

doe

doe thou deliver mee,
and from the men who meeagainst
my perſecuters bee.

(5)

15 Thy countenance for to ſhine forth
upon thy ſervant make:
o give to me ſalvation
even for thy mercy ſake.

17 Let me not be aſham'd, o Lord,
for cal'd on thee I have:
let wicked men be ſham'd,let them
be ſilent in the grave.

18 Let lying lips be ſilenced,
that againſt men upright
doe ſpeak ſuch things as greivous are,
in pride, & in deſpight.

19 How great 's thy goodnes, thou for the
that feare thee haſt hidden:
which thou work'ſt for them that thee truſt,
before the Sonnes of men.

20 Thou in the ſecretof thy face,
ſhalt hide them from mans pride:
in a pavillion, from the ſtrife
of tongues,thou wilt them hide.

21 O let Iehovah bleſſed be;
for he hath ſhewed mee
his loving kindnes wonderfull
in a fenced-cittie.

22 For I in haſt ſayd,I am caſt
from the ſight of thine eyes:
yet thou heard'ſt the voyce of my ſuit,

when

when to thee were my cryes.

23 O love the Lord all ye his Saints:
  becauſe the Lord doth guard
the faithfull, but the proud doer
  doth plenteouſly reward.

24 See that yee be encouraged,
  and let your heart wax ſtrong:
all whoſoever hopefully
  doe for Iehovah long.

32 A *pſalme* of David, Maſchil.

O Bleſſed is the man who hath
  his treſpaſſe pardoned,
and he *whoſe* aberration
  is wholly covered,

2 O bleſſed is the man to whom
  the Lord imputes not ſin:
and he who ſuch a ſpirit hath
  that guile is not therein.

3 When I kept ſilence then my bones,
  began to weare away,
with age; by meanes of my roaring
  continuing all the day.

4 For day & night thy hand on mee,
  heavily did indure:
into the drought of Summer time
  turned is my moiſture.   Selah.

5 Mine aberration unto thee
  I have acknowledged,
and mine iniquity I have
  not cloſely covered:
Againſt my ſelfe my ſin, ſayd I,

G

I will

I will to God confesse,
and thou didst the iniquitie
forgive of my trespasse.   Selah.

6 For this each godly one to thee
in finding time shall pray.
surely in floods of waters great,
come nigh him shall not they.

7 Thou art my hyding-place, thou shalt
from trouble save me out:
thou with songs of deliverance
shalt compasse me about.

8 I will instruct thee, also teach
thee in the way will I
which thou shalt goe: I will to thee
give counsell with mine eye.

9 Like to the horse & mule, which have
noe knowledge be not yee:
whose mouths are held with bridle-bir,
that come not neere to thee.

10 To those men that ungodly are,
their sorrows doe abound:
but him that trusteth in the Lord,
mercy shall compasse round.

11 Be in Iehovah joyfull yee,
yee righteous ones rejoyce;
and all that are upright in heart
shout yee with joyfull voyce.

psalme 33

YEe just in God rejoyce,
prayse well th'upright doth sute:
2 Prayse God with Harp, with psaltry sing

to him, on ten string'd lute.

3 Sing to him a new song,
    aloud play skilfully.

4 For the Lords word is right: and all
    his works in verity.

5 He loveth righteousnes,
    and also equity:
the earth replenished is with
    the Lords benignity.

6 By the word of the Lord
    the heavens had their frame,
and by the spirit of his mouth,
    all the host of the same.

7 The waters of the seas,
    he gathers as an heape;
together as in store-houses
    he layeth up the deepe.

8 Be all the earth in feare,
    because of Iehovah:
let all the dwellers of the world
    before him stand in awe.

9 Because he did but speak
    the word, & it was made:
he gave out the commandement,
    and it was firmly stay'd.

10 The Lord to nought doth bring
    the nations counsell; hee
devises of the people makes
    of none effect to bee.

11 The counsell of the Lord
    abide for ever shall,

G 2

the cogitations of his heart
to generations all.

(2)

12 O blessed nation,
    whose God Iehovah is:
and people whom for heritage
    chosen hee hath for his.

13 The Lord from heaven looks,
    all Sonnes of men views well.

14 From his firme dwelling hee looks forth,
    on all that on earth dwell.

15 The hearts of all of them
    alike he fashioneth:
and all their operations
    he well considereth.

16 By multitude of hoast
    there is no King saved:
nor is by multitude of strength
    the strong delivered.

17 A horse a vaine thing is
    to be a saviour:
nor shall he work deliverance
    by greatnes of his power.

18 On them that doe him feare
    loe, is Iehovahs eye:
upon them that doe place their hope
    on his benignity.

19 To save alive in dearth,
    and their soule from death free.

20 Our soule doth for Iehovah wayt,
    our help, & shield is hee.

21 for

21 For our heart joyes in him:
  for in's pure name trust wee.
22 Let thy mercy (Lord)be on us:
  like as we trust in thee.

Psalme 34

A *psalme* of David,whē he changed his behaviour
  before Abimelech,who drove him away
  & he departed.

I Le blesse God alwayes;his prayse shall
  still in my mouth be had.
2 My soule shall boast in God:the meeke
  shall heare *this* & bee glad.
3 Exalt the Lord with mee,his name
  let us together advance.
4 I sought,God heard, who gave from all
  my fears deliverance.
5 Him they beheld, & light'ned were,
  nor sham'd were their faces.
6 This poore man cry'd,the Lord him heard,
  and freed from all distresse.
7 His camp about them round doth pitch
  the Angell of the Lord;
  who doe him feare;and to them doth
  deliverance afford.
8 O tast,also consider yee,
  that God is good:o blest,
  that man is ever whose hope doth
  for safety in him rest.
9 O stand in feare of Iehovah,
  his holy ones who bee.
  because that such as doe him feare

G 3

not

not any want shall see.

10 The Lions young doe suffer lack,
  and suffer hungering:
  but they that seek Iehovah, shall
  not want any good thing.

(2)

11 I will you teach to feare the Lord:
  come children hark to mee.

12 Who is the man that willeth life:
  and loves good dayes to see?

13 Thy tongue from evill, & thy lips
  from speaking guile keep thou.

14 Depart from evill & doe good:
  seek peace, and it follow.

15 Vpon the men that righteous are
  the Lord doth set his eye:
  and likewise he doth bow his eare
  when unto him they cry.

16 Iehovahs face is set againſt
  them that doe wickedly:
  that he of them from off the earth
  may cut the memory.

17 They cry'd, God heard, & set them free,
  from their diſtreſſes all.

18 To broken hearts the Lord is neere,
  and contrite save he shall.

19 The juſt mans sorrows many are,
  from all God sets him free.

20 Hee kepeth all his bones, that none
  of them shall broken bee.

21 Evill shall certainly bring death
  the wicked man upon:

and

and thofe that hate the juft fhall come
   to defolation.

22 The foules of them that doe him ferve,
    Iehovah doth redeeme:
nor any fhall be defolate,
    that put their truft in him.

    35 *A pfalme* of David.

PLead, Lord, with them that with me plead:
    fight againft them that fight with mee.

2 Of fhield & buckler take thou hold,
   ftand up my helper for to bee.

3   Draw out the fpeare & ftop the way
   'gainft them that my purfuers bee:
   and doe thou fay unto my foule
   I am falvation unto thee.

4   Let them confounded be, & fham'd,
   that feek my foule how they may fpill:
   let them be turned back & fham'd
   that in their thoughts devife mine ill.

5   As chaffe before the winde, let them
   be, & Gods Angell them driving.

6 Let their way dark & flippery bee,
   and the Lords Angell them chafing.

7 For in a pit without a caufe,
   they hidden have for me a net:
   which they without a caufe have digg'd
   that they there in my foule may get.

9 Let unknowne ruin come on him,
   and let his net that he doth hide,
   himfelfe infnare: let him into
   the very fame deftruction flyde.

               6 My

9   My soule shall in the Lord be glad:
in his silvation joyfull bee

10 And all my bones shall also say,
o Lord, who is like unto thee?
   Who from the stronger then himselfe
the poore afflicted settest free:
the poore afflicted & needy,
from such as spoylers of him bee.

(2)

11 False witnesses did up arise:
what I knew not they charg'd on mee.

12 Evill for good they mee repay'd,
whereby my soule might spoyled bee,

13 But I, when they were sick, was cloath'd
with sackcloath, & I afflicted
my soule with fasting, & my pray'r
into my bosom returned.

14 I walked as if he had been
my neere freind or mine owne brother:
I heavily bow'd downe as one
that mourneth for his owne mother.

15 But they in mine adversity
rejoyced, & they gathered
themselves together: yea abjects
themselves against mee gathered;
   And I was ignorant *hereof*,
and they unceasantly mee teare,

16 With hypocrites, mockers in feasts;
at me their teeth they gnashing were.

17 How long o Lord wilt thou look on?
my soule from their destructions,

o doe

o doe thou set at liberty,
mine only one from the Lions.

18 I freely will give thanks to thee
within the congregation great:
and I thy prayses will set forth
where there be many people met.

19 Those that are wrongfully my foes,
let them not rejoyce over mee:
neither let them wink with the eye,
that are my haters causlesly.

20 Because that they doe not speak peace:
but in their thoughts they doe invent
deceitfull matters against them
that in the land for peace are bent.

21 Gainst me they op'ned their mouths wide,
& sayd, ah, ah our eye it saw.

22 Thou saw'st it (Lord) hold not thy peace:
Lord, from me be not far away.

23 Stirre up & wake to my judgement,
my God & my Lord, to my plea.

24 After thy justice, judge me, Lord
my God, lest or'e me joy should they.

25 Let them not say within their hearts,
aha, our soules desire have wee:
we now have swallowed him up,
o let them never say of mee.

25 Sham'd let them be & confounded
joyntly, who at my hurt are glad:
let them that 'gainst me magnify,
with shame & dishonour be clad.

27 Let them for joy shout, & be glad

H

that

that favour doe my righteous cause:
yea, let them say continually,
extolled be the Lord with prayse,
   Who doth in the prosperity
   of his servants his pleasure stay
23 And my tongue of thy justice shall,
   and of thy prayse speake all the day.

Psalme 36.

To the chief Musician a psalme of David,
   the servant of the Lord.

THe trespasse of the wicked one
   saith in assured-wise:
within my heart, the feare of God
   is not before his eyes.
2 For in his eyes he sooths himselfe:
   his sin is found meane while
3 hatefull. The words of his mouth are
   iniquity & guile:
He to be wise,to doe good leaves.
4   He mischief plotts on's bed,
he sets himselfe in way not good:
   he hath not ill hated.

       (2)
5 Thy mercy (Lord)in heaven is,
   to clouds thy faithfullnes.
6 Thy judgements a great deep, like great
   mountains thy righteousnes:
Thou savest man & beast,o Lord.
7   How pretious is thy grace,
therefore in shadow of thy wings
   mens sonnes their trust doe place.

                They

8 They of the fatnes of thy houſe
    unto the full ſhall take:
and of the river of thy joyes
    to drink thou ſhalt them make.

9 For with thee is the ſpring of life:
    in thy light wee'll ſee light.

10 To them that know thee ſtretch thy grace;
    to right in heart thy right.

11 Let no proud foot againſt me come,
    nor wicked hand move mee.

12 Wrong doers there are fal'n, caſt downe,
    and rayſ'd they cannot bee,

37 A Pſalme of David.

FRet not thy ſelfe becauſe of thoſe
    that evill workers bee,
nor envious bee againſt the men
    that work iniquitie.

2 For like unto the graſſe they ſhall
    be cut downe, ſuddenly:
and like unto the tender herb
    they withering ſhall dye.

3 Vpon the Lord put thou thy truſt,
    and bee thou doing good,
ſo ſhalt thou dwell within the land,
    and ſure thou ſhalt have food.

4 See that thou ſet thy hearts delight
    alſo upon the Lord,
and the deſyers of thy heart
    to thee he will afford.

5 Truſt in the Lord: & hee'l it work,
    to him commit thy way.

6 As

6 As light thy juſtice hee'l bring forth,
    thy judgement as noone day.

7 Reſt in Iehovah, & for him
    with patience doe thou ſtay:
  fret not thy ſelfe becauſe of him
    who proſpers in his way,
  Nor at the man, who brings to paſſe
    the crafts he doth deviſe.

8 Ceaſe ire, & wrath leave: to doe ill
    thy ſelfe fret in no wiſe.

9 For evil doers ſhall be made
    by cutting downe to fall:
  but thoſe that wayt upon the Lord,
    the land inherit ſhall.

(2)

10 For yet a litle while, & then
    the wicked ſhall not *bee*:
  yea, thou ſhalt diligently mark
    his place, & it not ſee.

11 But meek ones the inheritance
    ſhall of the earth poſſeſſe:
  alſo they ſhall themſelves delight
    in multitude of peace.

12 The wicked plotts againſt the juſt,
    gnaſhing at him his teeth.

13 The Lord ſhall laugh at him: becauſe
    his day coming he ſeeth.

14 The wicked have drawne out their ſword,
    & bent their bowe have they,
  to caſt the poor & needy downe,
    to kill th'upright in way.

15 their

15 Their sword shall enter their owne heart,
   their bowes shall broken bee.

16 The just mans little, better *is*
   then wickeds treasurie.

17 For th'armes of wicked shall be broke:
   the Lord the just doth stay.

18 The Lord doth know upright mens dayes:
   and their lot is for aye.

19 Neither shall they ashamed bee
   in any time of ill:
 and when the dayes of famine come,
   they then shall have their fill.

20 But wicked, & foes of the Lord
   as lambs fat shall decay:
 they shall consume:yea into smoake
   they shall consume away.

(3)

21 The man ungodly borroweth,
   but he doth not repay:
 but he that righteous is doth shew
   mercy,& gives away.

22 For such as of him blessed bee,
   the earth inherit shall,
 and they that of him cursed are,
   by cutting downe shall fall.

23 The foot-steps of a godly man
   they are by Iehovah
 established: & also hee
   delighteth in his way.

24 Although he fall,yet shall he not
   be utterly downe cast:

H 3   because

because Iehovah with his hand
   doth underprop him fast.
25 I have been young & now am old;
   yet have I never seen
the just man left, nor that his seed
   for bread have beggars been.
26 But every day hee's mercifull,
   and lends: his seed is blest.
27 Depart from evill,& doe good:
   and ever dwell at rest.
28 Because the Lord doth judgement love,
   his Saints forsakes not hee;
kept ever are they: but cut off
   the sinners seed shall bee.
29 The just inherit shall the land,
   and therein ever dwell.
30 The just mans mouth wisdome doth speak,
   his tongue doth judgement tell.
31 The law of his God is in's heart:
   none of his steps slideth.
32 The wicked watcheth for the just,
   and him to slay seeketh .
33 Iehovah will not such a one
   relinquish in his hand,
neither will he condemne him when
   adjudged he doth stand.
(4)
34 Wayt on the Lord,& keep his way,
   and hee shall thee exalt
th'earth to inherit: when cut off
   the wicked see thou shalt.

35 The

35 The wicked men I have beheld
 in mighty pow'r to bee:
also himsefe spreading abroad
 like to a green-bay-tree.

36 Neverthelesse he past away,
 and loe, then was not hee;
moreover I did seek for him,
 but found hee could not bee.

37 Take notice of the perfect man,
 and the upright attend:
because that unto such a man
 peace is his latter end.

38 But such men that transgressors are
 together perish shall:
the latter end shall be cut off
 of the ungodly all,

39 But the salvation of the just
 doth of Iehovah come:
he is their strength to them in times
 that are most troublesome.

40 Yea, help & free them will the Lord:
 he shall deliver them
from wiced men, because that they
 doe put their trust in him.

Psalme 38
A psalme of David,
to bring to remembrance.

LORD, in thy wrath rebuke me not:
 nor in thy hot rage chasten mee.

2 Because thine hand doth presse me sore:
 and in me thy shafts fastened bee.

3 Ther

3　　*There is* no soundnes in my flesh,
　　because thine anger I am in:
　　nor *is there* any rest within
　　my bones, by reason of my sin.

4　　　Because that mine iniquityes
　　ascended are above my head:
　　like as an heavy burden, they
　　to heavy upon me are layd.

5　　　My wounds stink, *and* corrupt they be:
　　my foolishnes doth make it so.

6　　I troubled am, & much bow'd downe,
　　all the day long I mourning goe.

7　　　For with foule sores my loynes are fill'd:
　　& in my flesh *is* no soundnes.

8　　I'me weak & broken sore; I roar'd
　　because of my hearts restlesnes.

9　　　All my desire's before thee, Lord;
　　nor is my groaning hid from thee.

10　My heart doth pant, my strength me fails:
　　& mine eye sight is gone from mee.

(2)

11　　My freinds & lovers from my sore
　　stand off: off stand my kinsmen eke.

12　And they lay snares that seek my life,
　　that seek my hurt, they mischief speak,
　　　And all day long imagin guile,

13　But as one deafe, I did not heare,
　　and as a dumb man I became
　　as if his mouth not open were.

14　　Thus was I as man that heares not,
　　& in whose mouth reproofes none were.

15 because

15 Becaufe o Lord, in thee I hope:
  o Lord my God, thou wilt mee heare.

16 For fayd I, left or'e me they joy:
  when my foot flips, they vaunt the more

17 themfelves 'gainft me. For I to halt
  am neere, my grief's ftill mee before.

18 For my tranfgreffion I'le declare;
  I for my fins will forry bee.

19 But yet my lively foes are ftrong,
  who falfly hate me, multiplie.

20 Moreover they that doe repay
  evill in ftead of good to mee,
  becaufe I follow what is good,
  to mee they adverfaryes bee.

21 Iehovah, doe not mee forfake:
  my God o doe not farre depart

22 from mee. Make haft unto mine ayd,
  o Lord who my falvation art.

Pfalme 39

To the chief mufician, *even* to Ieduthun,
a Pfalme of David.

I Sayd, I will look to my wayes,
  left I fin with my tongue:
  I'le keep my mouth with bit, while I
  the wicked am among.

2 With filence tyed was my tongue,
  my mouth I did refraine,
  From fpeaking that thing which is good,
  and ftirred was my paine.

3 Mine heart within me waxed hot,
  while I was mufing long,

I   inkindled

inkindled in me was the fire;
    then ſpake I with my tongue.

4 Mine end, o Lord, & of my dayes
    let mee the meaſure learne;
that what a momentany thing
    I am I may diſcerne.

5 Behold thou mad'ſt my dayes a ſpan,
    mine age as nought to thee:
ſurely each man at's beſt eſtate,
    is wholly vanity.   Selah.

6 Sure in a vaine ſhow walketh man;
    ſure ſtir'd in vaine they are:
he heaps up riches,& knows not
    who ſhall the ſame gather.

(2)

7 And now, o Lord what wayt I for?
    my hope is upon thee.

8 Free me from all my treſpaſſes:
    the fooles ſcorne make not mee.

9 I was dumb nor opned my mouth,
    this done becauſe thou haſt.

10 Remove thy ſtroke away fom mee:
    by thy hands blow I waſt.

11 When with rebukes thou doſt correct
    man for iniquity;
thou blaſt's his beauty like a moth:
    ſure each man 's vanity.   Selah.

12 Heare my pray'r, Lord, hark to my cry,
    be not ſtill at my tears:
for ſtranger, & pilgrim with thee,
    I 'me, as all my fathers.

13 O turne aside a while from mee,
    that I may strength recall:
before I doe depart from hence,
    and be noe more at all.

Psalme 40.

To the chief musician, a psalme
of David.

VVIth expectation for the Lord
    I wayted patiently,
and hee inclined unto mee.
    also he heard my cry.

2 He brought mee out of dreadfull-pit,
    out of the miery clay:
and set my feet upon a rock,
    hee stablished my way.

3 And in my mouth put a new song,
    of prayse our God unto:
many shall see, & feare, upon
    the Lord shall trust also.

4 Blest is the man that on the Lord
    maketh his trust abide:
nor doth the proud respect, nor such
    to lies as turne aside.

5 O thou Iehovah, thou my God,
    hast many a wonder wrought:
and likewise towards us thou hast
    conceived many a thought.
Their summe cannot be reck'ned up'
    in order unto thee:
would I declare & speak *of them*,
    beyond account they bee.

I 2
        6 Thou

(2)

6 Thou sacrifice & offering
    wouldst not; thou boar'st mine eare:
  burnt offring, & sin offering
    thou neither didst requere.

7 Then sayd I: loe, I come: ith books
    rolle it is writt of mee.

8 To doe thy will, God, I delight:
    thy laws in my heart bee.

9 In the great congregation
    thy righteousnes I show:
  loe, I have not refraynd my lips,
    Iehovah, thou dost know.

10 I have not hid thy righteousnes
    within my heart alone:
  I have declar'd thy faithfullnes
    and thy salvation:
  Thy mercy nor thy truth have I
    from the great Church conceald.

11 Let not thy tender mercyes bee
    from mee o Lord with-held.
  Let both thy kindnes & thy truth
    keep me my life throughout.

12 Because innumerable ills
    have compast mee about:
  My sins have caught me so that I
    not able am to see:
  more are they then hairs of my head,
    therefore my heart fails mee

(3)

13 Be pleas'd Lord, to deliver mee

to help me Lord make haſt.

14 At once abaſht & ſham'd let bee
who ſeek my ſoule to waſte:
Let them be driven back,& ſham'd,
that wiſh me miſery.

15 Let them be waſte, to quit their ſhame,
that ſay to me,fy fy.

16 Let all be glad, & joy in thee,
that ſeek thee: let them ſay
who thy ſalvation love, the Lord
be magnifyde alway.

17 I both diſtreſt & needy am,
the Lord *yet* thinks on mee:
my help & my deliverer thou
my God, doe not tarry.

Pſalme 41
To the chief muſician, a pſalme
of David.

Bleſſed is hee that wiſely doth
unto the poore attend:
the Lord will him deliverance
in time of trouble ſend.

2 Him God will keep, & make to live,
on earth hee bleſt ſhall be,
nor doe thou him unto the will
give of his enemie.

3 Vpon the bed of languiſhing,
the Lord will ſtrengthen him:
thou alſo wilt make all his bed
within his ſicknes time.

4 I ſayd, Iehouah, o be thou

I 3

merciful

mercifull unto mee;
heale thou my soule, because that I
have sinned against thee.

5 Those men that be mine enemies,
with evill mee defame:
when will the time come hee shall dye,
and perish shall his name?

6 And if he come to see *mee*, hee
speaks vanity: his heart
sin to it selfe heaps, when hee goes
forth hee doth it impart.

(2)

7 All that me hate, against mee they
together whisper still:
against me they imagin doe
to mee malicious ill.

8 *Thus doe they say* some ill disease,
unto him cleaveth sore:
and *seing now* he lyeth downe,
he shall rise up noe more.

9 Moreover my familiar freind,
on whom my trust I set,
his heele against mee lifted up,
who of my bread did eat.

10 But Lord me pitty, & mee rayse,
that I may them requite.

11 By this I know assuredly,
in mee thou dost delight:
For o're mee triumphs not my foe.

12 And mee, thou dost mee stay,
in mine integrity; & set'st

mee

mee thee before for aye.
13 Bleſt hath Iehovah Iſraels God
    from everlaſting *been*,
 alſo unto everlaſting:
    Amen, yea and Amen.

THE

SECOND BOOKE.

PSALME 42
To the chief muſician, *Maſchil*, for the
    Sonnes of Korah.

Like as the Hart panting doth bray
    after the water brooks,
 even in ſuch wiſe o God, my ſoule,
    after thee panting looks.
2 For God, even for the liuing God,
    my ſoule it thirſteth ſore:
 oh when ſhall I come & appeare,
    the face of God before.
3 My teares have been unto mee meat,
    by night alſo by day,
 while all the day they unto mee
    where is thy God doe ſay.
4 When as I doe in minde record
    theſe things, then me upon
 I doe my ſoule out poure, for I
    with multitude had gone:
 With them unto Gods houſe I went,
    with voyce of joy & prayſe:

                               I with

I with a multitude did goe
    that did keepe-holy-days.
5 My soule why art cast downe?& art
    stirr'd in mee: thy hope place
in God, for yet him prayse I shall
    for the help of his face.

(2)

6 My God, my soule in mee's cast downe,
    therefore thee minde I will
from Iordanes & Hermonites land,
    and from the litle hill.

7 At the noyse of thy water spouts
    deep unto deep doth call:
thy waves they are gone over mee,
    also thy billowes all.

8 His loving kindnes yet the Lord
    command will in the day:
a nd in the night his song with mee,
    to my lifes God I'le pray.

9 I unto God will say, my Rock
    why hast thou forgot mee?
why goe I sad, by reason of
    pressure of th' enemie.

10 As with a sword within my bones
    my foes reproach mee do:
while all the day, where is thy God?
    they doe say mee unto.

11 My soule o wherefore dost thou bowe
    thy selfe downe heavily;
and wherefore in mee makest thou
    a stirr tumultuously?

Hope

Hope thou in God, becauſe I ſhall
    with prayſe him yet advance:
who is my God, alſo he is
    health of my countenance.

Pſalme 43.

IVdge me, o God, & plead my cauſe
    from nation mercyleſſe;
from the guilefull & man unjuſt,
    o ſend thou me redreſſe.

2 For of my ſtrength thou art the God,
    why caſt's thou mee thee fro:
why goe I mourning for the ſore
    oppreſſion of the foe?

3 Thy light o ſend out & thy truth,
    let them lead, & bring mee,
unto thy holy hill, & where
    thy tabernacles bee.

4 Then will I to Gods Altar goe,
    to God my joyes gladnes:
upon the Harp o God my God
    I will thy prayſe expreſſe.

5 My ſoule o wherfore doſt thou bowe
    thy ſelfe downe heavily;
and wherefore in mee makeſt thou
    a ſtirre tumultuouſly?
Hope thou in God, becauſe I ſhall
    with prayſe him yet advance:
who is my God, alſo he is
    health of my countenance.

Pſalme 44

    To the chief muſician, for the ſonnes-
of Korah.   K   PSAL-

PSALM xliv.

WEE with our eares have heard, o God,
    our fathers have us told,
what works thou diddest in their dayes,
    in former dayes of old.

2 *How* thy hand drave the heathen out,
    and them thou planted hast;
how thou the people didst afflict,
    and thou didst them out-cast.

3 For they got not by their owne sword
    the lands possession,
neither yet was it their owne arme
    wrought their salvation:
But thy right hand, thine arme also,
    thy countenances light;
because that of thine owne good will
    thou didst in them delight.

4 Thou art my king, o mighty God,
    thou dost the same indure:
doe thou for Iacob by command
    deliverances procure.

5 Through thee as with a horne wee will
    push downe our enemies:
through thy name will wee tread them downe
    that up against us rise.

6 Because that I will in no wise
    any affiance have,
upon my bow, neither is it
    my sword that shall mee save.

7 But from our enemies us thou sav'd,
    and put our foes to shame.

8 In God wee boast all the day long,

                 and

and for aye prayse thy name.   Selah.

(2)

9 But thou hast cast us off away,
    thou makest us also
to be asham'd; neither dost thou
    forth with our armies goe.

10 Vs from before the enemy
    thou makest back recoyle:
likewise they which our haters bee,
    for themselves us doe spoyle.

11 Thou hast us given like to sheep
    to slaughter *that belong*:
also thou hast us scattered
    the heathen folk among.

12 Thou dost thy people set to sale
    whereby no wealth doth rise:
neither dost thou obtaine increase
    of riches by their price.

13 Vnto our neighbours a reproach
    thou doest us expose,
a scorne we are & mocking stock,
    to them that us inclose.

14 Among the heathen people thou
    a by word dost us make:
also among the nations,
    at us their heads they shake.

15 Before me my confusion
    it is continually,
and of my countenance the shame
    hath over covered mee.

16 Because of his voyce that doth scorne,

and scoffingly despight:
by reason of the enemy,
    and selfe revenging wight.

(3)

17 All this is come on us, wee yet
    have not forgotten thee:
neither against thy covenant
    have wee dealt faithleslie.

18 Our heart is not turn'd back, nor have
    our steps from thy way stray'd;

19 Though us thou brake in dragons place,
    and hid us in deaths shade.

20 had wee forgot Gods name, or stretcht
    to a strange God our hands:

21 Shall not God search this out? for hee
    hearts secrets understands.

22 Yea, for thee all day wee are kil'd:
    counted as sheep to slay.

23 Awake, why sleepst thou, Lord? arise,
    cast us not off for aye.

24 Thy countenance away from us
    o wherefore dost thou hide?
of our grief & oppression
    forgetfull dost abide.

25 For our soule is bowd downe to dust:
    to earth cleaves our belly.

26 Rise for our help, & us redeeme,
    because of thy mercy.

Psalme 45

To the chief musician upon Shoshannim, for
the sonnes of Korah, Maschil a song of loves.

PSAL.

MY heart good mater boyleth forth,
 my works touching the King
I speak: my tongue is as the pen
 of Scribe swiftly writing.

2 Fairer thou art then sonnes of men,
 grace in thy lips is shed:
because of this the Lord hath thee
 for evermore blessed.

3 Thy wasting sword o mighty one
 gird thou upon thy thigh:
thy glorious-magnificence,
 and comely majesty.

4 Ride forth upon the word of truth,
 meeknes & righteousnes:
and thy right hand shall lead thee forth
 in works of dreadfulnes.

5 Within the heart of the kings foes
 thine arrows piercing bee:
whereby the people overcome,
 shall fall downe under thee.

6 Thy throne o God, for ever is,
 the scepter of thy state

7 right scepter is. Iustice thou lov'st,
 but wickednes dost hate:
Because of this, God ev'n thy God
 hee hath annoynted thee,
with oyle of gladnes above them,
 that thy companions bee.

8 Myrrhs, Aloes, and Cassias *smell*,
 all of thy garments *had*:
out of the yvory pallaces

they

wherby they made thee glad.

9 Amongſt thine honourable maids
    kings daughters preſent were,
the Queen is ſet at thy right hand
    in fine gold of Ophir.

(2)

10 Harken o daughter, & behold,
    doe thou incline thine eare:
doe thou forget thine owne people,
    and houſe of thy father.

11 So ſhall the king delighting-reſt
    himſelfe in thy beautie:
and bowing downe worſhip thou him,
    becauſe thy Lord is hee.

12 Then ſhall be preſent with a gift
    the daughter there of Tyre:
the wealthy ones of the people
    thy favour ſhall deſire.

13 The daughter of the king ſhe is
    all glorious within:
and with imbroderies of gold,
    her garments wrought have been.

14 She is led in unto the king
    in robes with needle wrought:
the virgins that doe follow her
    ſhall unto thee be brought.

15 They ſhall be brought forth with gladnes,
    alſo with rejoycing,
ſo ſhall they entrance have into
    the Pallace of the king.

16 Thy children ſhall inſtead of thoſe
    that were thy fathers bee:

whom

whom thou mayſt place in all the earth
    in princely diginty.
17 Thy name remembred I will make
    through generations all:
therefore for ever & for aye
    the people prayſe thee ſhall.

Pſalme 46

To the chief muſician, for the ſonnes of-
    Korah, a ſong upon Alemoth.

GOD is our refuge, ſtrength, & help
    in troubles very neere.
2 Therefore we will not be afrayd,
    though th'earth removed were.
Though mountaines move to midſt of ſeas
3   Though waters roaring make
and troubled be, at whoſe ſwellings
    although the mountaines ſhake.   Selah.
4 There is a river ſtreames whereof
    ſhall rejoyce Gods city:
the holy place the tent wherin
    abideth the moſt high.
5 God is within the midſt of her,
    moved ſhee ſhall not bee:
God ſhall be unto her an help,
    in the morning early.
6 The nations made tumultuous noyſe,
    the kingdomes moved were:
he did give forth his thundering voyce
    the earth did melt *with feare.*
7 The God of Armies is with us
    th'eternall Iehovah:

the

the God of Iacob is for us
a refuge high. Selah.

8 O come yee forth behold the works
which Iehovah hath wrought,
the fearfull defolations,
which on the earth he brought.

9 Vnto the utmoft ends of th'earth
warres into peace hee turnes:
the fpeare he cuts, the bowe he breaks,
in fire the chariots burnes.

10 Be ftill, & know that I am God,
exalted be will I
among the heathen: through the earth
I 'le be exalted hye.

11 The God of armyes is with us,
th'eternall Iehovah:
the God of Iacob is for us
a refuge high. Selah.

Pfalme 47.

To the chief muſician: a pſalme for the
Sonnes of Korah.

CLap hands all people, fhout for joy,
to God with voyce of finging mirth:

2 For high Iehovah fearfull is,
a great King over all the earth.

3 People to us he doth fubdue,
and nations under our feet lay.

4 For us our heritage he chofe,
his deare Iacobs glory. Selah.

5 God is afcended with a fhout:
Iehovah with the trumpets noyfe.

6 Sing

6 Sing psalmes to God, sing psalmes, sing-
unto our King with singing voyce.   (psalmes
7   For God is King of all the earth,
sing yee psalmes of instruction :
8 Over the heathen God will reigne
God sits his holy throne upon.
9   To the people of Abrahams-God
Princes of peoples gathered bee,
for shields of th'earth to God belong:
he is exalted mightylie.

Psalme 48
To the chief musician, a song & psalme for
the sonnes of Korah.

GReat is Iehovah, & he is
to be praysed greatly
within the city of our God,
in his mountaine holy.
2 For situation beautifull,
the joy of the whole earth
mount Sion; the great Kings city
on the sides of the north.
3 God in her pallaces is knowne
to be a refuge high.
4 For loe, the kings assembled were:
they past together by.
5 They saw, & so they merveiled,
were troubled, fled for feare.
6 Trembling seiz'd on them there & paine
like her that childe doth beare.
7 The navies that of Tarshish are
in pieces thou breakest:

L   even

ev'n with a very blaſt of winde
   coming out of the eaſt.
8 As we heard, ſo we ſaw within
   the Lord of hoaſts citty,
in our Gods citty, God will it
   ſtabliſh eternally.   Selah.

(2)

9 O God we have had thoughts upon
   thy free benignity,
within the very midle part
   of thy temple holy,
10 According to thy name, o God
   ſo is thy prayſe unto
the ends of earth: thy right hand 's full
   of righteouſnes alſo.
11 Let the mountaine Sion rejoyce,
   and triumph let them make
who are the daughters of Iudah,
   ev'n for thy judgements ſake.
12 About the hill of Sion walk,
   and goe about her yee,
and doe yee reckon up thereof
   the tow'rs *that therein* bee.
13 Doe yee full well her bulwarks mark,
   her Pallaces view well,
that to the generation
   to come yee may it tell.
14 For this ſame God he is our God
   for ever & for aye:
likewiſe unto the very death
   he guides us in our way.

PSALM

Psalme 49

To the chief mufician a pfalme for the
fonnes of Korah.

HEare this all people, all give eare
that dwell the world all o're.

2 Sonnes both of low, & higher men,
joyntly both rich & poore.

3 My mouth it fhall variety
of wifdome be fpeaking:
and my hearts meditation fhall
be of underftanding.

4 Vnto a fpeech proverbiall
I will mine eare incline;
I will alfo upon the Harp
open my dark doctrine.

5 Why fhould I be at all afrayd
in dayes that evill bee:
when that my heeles iniquity
about fhall compaffe mee.

(2)

6 Thofe men that make their great eftates
their ftay to truft unto,
who in the plenty of their wealth
themfelves doe boaft alfo:

7 Ther 's not a man *of them* that can
by any meanes redeeme
his brother, nor give unto God
enough to ranfome him.

8 So deare their foules redemption is
& ever ceafeth it.

L 2

9 That

9 That he should still for ever live
    and never see the pit.
10 For he doth see that wise man dye,
    the foole and brutish too
to perish, & their rich estate
    to others leave they doo.
11 They think their houses are for aye
    to generations all
their dwelling places, & their lands
    by their owne names they call.
12 Neverthelesse, in honour man,
    abideth not a night:
become he is just like unto
    the beasts that perish quite.
13 This their owne way their folly is;
    yet whatsoe're they say,
their successors that follow them
    doe well approve. Selah.
14 Like sheep so are they layd in grave,
    death shall them feed upon;
& th' upright over them in morn
    shall have dominion.
And from the place where they doe dwell,
    the beauty which they have,
shall utterly consume away
    in the devouring grave.
(3)
15 But surely Gods redemption
    unto my soule will give,
even from the power of the grave,
    for he will me receive.   Selah.

16 Be not afrayd when as a man
    in wealth is made to grow,
and when the glory of his house
    abundantly doth flow.

17 Because he shall carry away
    nothing when he doth dye:
neither shall after him descend
    ought of his dignity.

18 And albeit that he his soule
    in time of his life blest,
and men will prayse thee, when as thou
    much of thy selfe makest.

19 He shall goe to his fathers race,
    they never shall see light.

20 Man in honour, & know'th not, is
    like beasts that perish quite.

Psalme 50.
A psalme of Asaph.

THe mighty God, the Lord hath spoke,
    and he the earth doth call,
from the uprising of the Sun,
    thereof unto the fall.

2 The mighty God hath clearely shyn'd
    out of the mount Sion,
which is of beauty excellent
    the full perfection.

3 Our God shall come, and not be still
    fire shall waste in his sight;
and round about him shall be rays'd
    a storme of vehement might.

4 His folk to judge he from above

calls

calls heavens,& earth likewise,

5 Bring mee my Saints,that cov'nant make
 with mee by sacrifice.

6 And the heavens shall his righteousnes
 shew forth apparentlie:
because the mighty God himselfe
 a righteous judge will bee.   Selah.

(2)

7 Heare, o my people,& I will
 speake,I will testify
also to thee o Israell,
 I even thy God am I.

8 As for thy sacrifices I
 will finde no fault with thee,
or thy burnt offrings,*which have been*
 at all times before mee.

9 Ile take no bullocks,nor he-goates
 from house,or foldes of thine.

10 For forrest beasts,& cattell all
 on thousand hills are mine.

11 The flying foules of the mountaines
 all of them doe I know:
and every wilde beast of the field
 it is with mee also.

12 If I were hungry I would not
 it unto thee declare:
for mine the habitable world,
 and fullnes of it *are*.

13 Of bullocks eate the flesh,or drink
 the blood of goates will I ?

14 Thanks offer unto God,& pay

           thy

thy vowes to the moſt high.
15 And in the day of trouble ſore
    doe thou unto mee cry,
and I will thee deliver, and
    thou mee ſhalt glorify.

(3)

16 But to the wicked God ſayth, why
    doſt thou the mention make
of my ſtatutes, why in thy mouth
    ſhould'ſt thou my cov'nant take?
17 Sith thou doſt hate teaching and doſt
    my words behinde thee caſt.
18 When thou didſt ſee a thief, then thou
    with him conſented haſt;
And likewiſe with adulterers
    thy part hath been the ſame.
19 Thy mouth to evill thou doſt give,
    and guile thy tongue doth frame,
Thou ſitteſt, thou doſt ſpeake againſt
    the man that is thy brother:
and thou doſt ſlaunder him that is
    the ſonne of thine owne mother.
21 Theſe things haſt thou committed, and
    in ſilence I kept cloſe:
that I was altogether like
    thy ſelfe, thou didſt ſuppoſe:
I'le thee reprove, & in order
    before thine eyes them ſet.
22 O therefore now conſider this
    yee that doe God forget:
Leſt I you teare, & there be not

any

any deliverer.

23 He glorifieth mee that doth
    prayſe unto mee offer.

24 And hee that doth order *aright*
    his converſation,
to him will I give that hee may
    ſee Gods ſalvation.

Pſalme 51.

To the chief muſician, a pſalme of David, when
Nathan the prophet came unto him, after he
had gone in unto Bathſheba.

HAve mercy upon mee o God,
   in thy loving kyndnes:
in multitude of thy mercyes
    blot out my treſpaſſes.

2 From mine iniquity doe thou
    waſh mee moſt perfectly,
and alſo from this ſin of mine
    doe thou mee puriſy.

3 Becauſe, of my tranſgreſſions
    my ſelfe doe take notice,
and ſin that I committed have
    before mee ever is.

4 Gainſt thee, thee only I have ſin'd
    this ill done thee before:
when thou ſpeakſt juſt thou art, & cleare
    when thou doſt judge therfore.

5 Behold, how in iniquity
    I did my ſhape receive:
alſo my mother *that mee bare*
    in ſin did mee conceive.

6 Behold

6 Behold, thou dost desire the truth
within the inward part:
and thou shalt make mee wisdome know
in secret of my heart.

7 With hysope doe me purify,
I shall be cleansed so:
doe thou mee wash, & then I shall
be whiter then the snow.

8 Of joy & of gladnes doe thou
make me to heare the voyce:
that so the bones which thou hast broke
may cheerfully rejoyce.

9 From the beholding of my sin
hide thou away thy face:
also all mine iniquityes
doe utterly deface.

(2)

10 A cleane heart (Lord) in me create,
also a spirit right

11 in me renew. O cast not mee
away out of thy sight;
Nor from me take thy holy spirit.

12 Restore the joy to mee
of thy salvation, & uphold
me with thy spirit free.

13 Then will I teach thy wayes to those
that work iniquitie:
and by this meanes shall sinners bee
converted unto thee.

14 O God, God of my health, set mee
free from bloud guiltines,

M

and

and so my tongue shall joyfully
    sing of thy righteousnes.
15 O Lord-my-stay, let thou my lips
    by thee be opened,
    and by my mouth thy prayses shall
    be openly shewed.
16 For thou desir'st not sacrifice,
    it would I freely bring:
    neither dost thou contentment take
    in a whole burnt offring.
17 The sacrifices of the Lord
    they are a broken sprite:
    God, thou wilt not despise a heart
    that's broken, & contrite.
13 In thy good pleasure o doe thou
    doe good to Sion hill:
    the walles of thy Ierusalem
    o doe thou build up still.
19 The sacrifice of justice shall
    please thee, with burnt offring,
    and whole burnt offring; then they shall
    calves to thine Altar bring.

Another of the same.

O GOD, have mercy upon mee,
    according to thy kindenes deare:
and as thy mercyes many bee,
    quite doe thou my transgressions cleare.
2   From my perversues mee wash through,
    and from my sin mee purify.
3 For my transgressions I doe know,

before

before mee is my sin dayly.

4   Gainſt thee, thee only sin'd have I,
  & done this evill in thy sight:
  that when thou speakſt thee juſtify
  men may, and judging cleare thee quite.

5   Loe, in injuſtice ſhape't I was:
  in sin my mother conceav'd mee.

6   Loe, thou in th'inwards truth lov'd haz:
  and made mee wise in secrecie.

7   Purge me with hyſſope, & I cleare
  ſhall be; mee waſh, & then the ſnow

8   I ſhall be whiter. Make me heare
  Ioy & gladnes, the bones which ſo
    Thou broken haſt joy cheerly ſhall.

9   Hyde from my sins thy face away
  blot thou iniquityes out all
  which are upon mee any way.

(2)

10   Create in mee cleane heart *at laſt*
  God: a right ſpirit in me new make.

11   Nor from thy presence quite me caſt,
  thy holy ſpright nor from me take.

12   Mee thy salvations joy reſtore,
  and ſtay me with thy ſpirit free.

13   I wil, tranſgreſſors teach thy lore,
  and sinners ſhall be turnd to thee.

14   Deliver mee from guilt of bloud,
  o God, God of my health-ſaving,
  which if thou ſhalt vouchſafe, aloud
  thy righteouſnes my tongue ſhall sing.

15   My lips doe thou, o Lord, uncloſe,

and

and thy prayſe ſhall my mouth forth ſhowe

16 For ſacrifice thou haſt not choſe,
that I ſhould it on thee beſtow:
   Thou joy'ſt not in burnt ſacrifice.

17 Gods ſacrifices are a ſp'ryte
broken; o God, thou'lt not deſpiſe,
   a heart that's broken & contrite.

18   In thy good will doe thou beſtow
on Sion goodnes bounteouſlie:
   Ieruſalems walles that lye ſo low
   doe thou vouchſafe to edifie.

19   Then ſhalt thou pleaſe to entertaine
the ſacrifices with content
of righteouſnes, the offrings ſlaine,
which unto thee wee ſhall preſent,

   Together with the offerings
ſuch as in fire whole burned are:
   and then they ſhall their bullocks bring,
   offrings to be on thine altar.

Pſalme 52

To the chief muſician, Maſchil. a pſalme of
David: when Doeg the Edomite came and
told Saule, & ſayd unto him, Dauid is
come to the houſe of Ahimilech.

O Man of might, wherefore doſt thou
   thus boaſt thy ſelfe in ill?
the goodnes of the mighty God
   endureth ever ſtill.

2 Thy tongue preſumptuouſly doth
miſchievous things deviſe:
   it is like to a razor ſharp,

             working

working deceitfull lies.

3 Thou lovest evil more then good,
　more to speak lies then right.
4 O guilefull tongue, thou dost in all
　devouring words delight.
5 God shall likewise for evermore
　destroying thee deface,
he shall take thee away, & pluck
　thee from thy dwelling place,
And also root thee out from off
　the land of the living.　　Selah.
6 The righteous also shall it see
　and feare, at him laughing.
7 Loe, this the man *that* made not God
　his strength: but trusted in
his store of wealth, himselfe made strong
　in his mischievous sin.
8 But in the house of God *am* I
　like a greene Olive-tree:
I trust for ever & for aye,
　in Gods benignitie.
9 Thee will I prayse for evermore,
　because thou hast done this:
and I'le wayt on thy name, for good
　before thy Saints that is.

Psalme 53.

To the chief musician upon Mahalath,
　Maschil. a *psalme* of David.

THe foole in's heart saith, *there's* no God;
　they are corrupt, have done
abominable practises;

M 3　　　　　　　　that

that doth good there is none.

2 The Lord from heaven looked downe
   on sonnes of men, to see
  if any that doth understand,
   that seeketh God there bee.

3 All are gone back, together they
   ev'n filthy are become:
  and there is none that doeth good,
   noe not so much as one.

4 The workers of iniquityes
   have they noe knowledge all?
  who eate my people: they eate bread;
   and on God doe not call.

5 Greatly they fear'd, *where* noe feare was,
   'gainst thee in camp that lyes
  his bones God scattered; & them sham'd
   for God doth *them* despise.

6 Who Israells health from Sion gives?
   his folks captivitie
  when God shall turne: Iacob shall joye
   glad Israell shall bee.

Psalme 54

To the chief musician on Neginoth, Maschil, *a
psalme* of David, when the Ziphims came & sayd
to Saul, doth not David hide himselfe with us?

PReserve mee, by thy name, o God,
   & by thy strength judge mee.

2 O God, my pray'r heare, give eare to
   words in my mouth that bee.

3 For strangers up against me rise,
   and who oppresse me sore,

                       pursue

pursue my soule; neither have they
    set God themselves before.   Selah.

4 Loe, God helps mee, the Lord's with them
    that doe my soule sustaine.

5 He shall reward ill to my foes:
    them in thy truth restrayne.

6 Vnto thee sacrifice will I,
    with voluntarines;
Lord, to thy name I will give prayse,
    because of thy goodnes.

7 For he hath mee delivered,
    out of all miseryes:
and i:s desire mine eye hath seen
    upon mine enemyes.

Psalme 55

To the chief musician on Neginoth, Maschil,
    a psalme of David.

O GOD, doe thou give eare unto
    my supplication:
and doe not hide thy selfe away
    from my petition.

2 Bee thou attentive unto mee,
    and answer mee returne,
I in my meditation
    doe make a noyse & mourne.

3 Because of th'enemies voyce, because
    the wicked haue opprest,
for they injustice on mee cast
    and in wrath mee detest.

4 My heart in mee is payn'd, on mee
    deaths terrors fallen bee.

                      5 Trembling

5 Trembling & feare are on mee come,
    horrour hath covered mee.
6 Then did I say,o who to mee
    wings of a dove will give;
  that I might flie away & might
    in quiet dwelling live.
7 *Loe*,I would wander farre away,
    and in the desart rest.   Selah,
8 Soone would I scape from windy storme,
    from violent tempest.

(2)

9 Lord bring on them destruction,
    doe thou their tongues divide;
  for strife & violence I within
    the city have espy'd.
10 About it on the walles thereof,
    they doe walk night & day:
  mischief also & sorrow doe
    in middest of it stay.
11 In midst thereof there's wickednes;
    deceitfullnes also,
  and out of the broad streets thereof
    guilefullnes doth not go.
12 For t'was no foe reproacht mee,then
    could I have borne; nor did
  my foe against me lift himselfe
    from him had I me hid.
13 But thou it was,the man that wert
    my well esteemed peere,
  which wast to mee my speciall guide,
    and mine acquaintance neere.

14 Wee did together counſell take
    in ſweet ſociety:
  and wee did walk into the houſe
    of God in company.

15 Let death ſeize on them,& let them
    goe downe quick into hell:
  for wickednes among them is
    in places where they dwell.

(2)

16 As for mee, I will call on God;
    and mee the Lord ſave ſhall.

17 Ev'ning morn,& at noon will I
    pray, & aloud will call,

18 and he ſhall heare my voyce. He hath
    in peace my ſoule ſet free
  from warre that was 'gainſt mee,becauſe
    there many were with mee.

19 God ſhall heare,& them ſmite,ev'n he
    that doth of old abide;   Selah.
  becauſe they have no change,therefore
    Gods feare they lay aſide.

20 Gainſt ſuch as be at peace with him
    hee hath put forth his hand:
  he hath alſo the covenant
    which he had made prophan'd.

21 His words then butter ſmoother were,
    but warre in's heart:his words
  more then the oyle were ſoftened
    but yet they were drawne ſwords.

22 Thy burden caſt upon the Lord,
    and he ſuſtaine thee ſhall:

N   nor

nor shall he suffer righteous ones
    to be remov'd at all.

23 But thou o God, shalt downe to hell
    bring them who bloody bee,
  guilefull shall not live halfe their dayes:
    but I will trust in thee.

Psalme 56.

To the chief musician upõ Ionath Elem Recho-
-kim, Michtam of David, when the Philistims
tooke him in Gath.

LORD, pitty mee, because
  man would up swallow mee:
and fighting all the day throughout,
    oppresse mee sore doth hee.

2 Mine enemies they would
    me swallow up dayly;
for they *be* many that doe fight
    against mee, o most high.

3 I'le put my trust in thee,
    what time I am afrayd.

4 In God I'le prayse his word, in God
    my confidence have stayd;
I will not be afrayd
    what flesh can doe to mee.

5 All day they wrest my words: their thoughts
    for ill against me bee.

6 They joyne themseves together;
    themselves they closely hyde;
they mark my steps when for my soule
    wayting they doe abyde.

7 Shall they make an escape

by their iniquity;
thou in thine anger downe depresse
the folk, o God mighty.

8 My wandrings thou dost tell,
    put thou my weeping teares
into thy bottle; *are* they not
    within thy registers.

9 Then shall my foes turne back,
    when I crye unto thee:
this I doe know assuredly,
    because God is for mee.

10 In God I'le prayse his word:
    the Lords word I will prayse.

11 In God I trust: I will not feare
    what man 'gainst mee can rayse.

12 Thy vowes on me o God;
    I'le render prayse to thee.

13 Because that thou my soule from death
    delivering dost free;
Deliver wilt not thou
    my feet from downe falling?
so that I may walk before God
    ith light of the living.

Psalme 57

To the chief musician Altaschith, Michtam of
David, when he fled from Saul in the cave.

O GOD, to me be mercifull,
    be mercifull to mee:
because my soule for shelter-safe
    betakes it selfe to thee.
Yea in the shaddow of thy wings,
    my refuge I have plac't,   N 2   until

untill these sore calamities
   shall quite be over past.
2 To God most high I cry:the God
   that doth for me performe.
3 He will from heaven send, & save
   mee from the spightfull scorne
Of him that would with greedy hast,
   swallow me vtterly: Selah.
the Lord from heaven will send forth
   his grace & verity.
4 My soule's 'mongst lions, & I lye
   with men on-fier-set:
mens sonnes whose teeth are spears,& shafts,
   whose tongues as swords are whet.
5 O God,doe thou exalt thy selfe,
   above the heavens high:
up over all the earth also
   lifted be thy glory.
6 They for my steps prepar'd a net,
   my soule is bow'd; a pit
they dig'd before me, but *themselves*
   are fall'n in midst of it.   Selah.
7 My heart o God, prepared is,
   prepared is my heart,
sing will I, & sing prayse with psalmes.
8 Vp o my glorie start;
Wake Psaltery & Harp, I will
   awake in the morning.
9 Among the folk I'le prayse thee,Lord,
   'mongst nations to thee sing.

10 For great unto the heavens is
thy mercifull bounty:
thy verity also doth reach
unto the cloudy skye.

11 O God, doe thou exalt thy selfe,
above the heavens high:
up over all the earth also
lifted *be* thy glory.

Psalme 58

To the chief musician, Altaschi:h,
michtam of David.

DOe yee o congregation,
indeed speak righteousnes?
and o yee sons of earthly men,
doe yee judge uprightnes?

2 Yea you in heart will working be
injurious-wickednes;
and in the land you will weigh out
your hands violentnes.

3 The wicked are estranged from
the womb, they goe astray
as soone as ever they are borne;
uttering lyes are they.

4 Their poyson's like serpents poyson:
they like deafe Aspe, her eare

5 that stops. Though Charmer wisely charme,
his voice she will not heare.

6 Within their mouth doe thou their teeth
break out, o God most strong,
doe thou Iehovah, the great teeth
break of the lions young.

N 3   7 As

7 As waters let them melt away,
    that run continually:
  and when he bends his shafts, let them
    as cut asunder bee.

8 Like to a snayle that melts, so let
    each of them passe away;
  like to a womans untimely birth
    see Sun that neuer they may.

9 Before your potts can feele the thornes,
    take them away shall hee,
  as with a whirlwinde both living,
    and in his jealousee.

10 The righteous will rejoyce when as
    the vengeance he doth see:
  his feet wash shall he in the blood
    of them that wicked bee.

11 So that a man shall say, surely
    for righteous there is fruit:
  sure there's a God that in the earth
    judgement doth execute.

Psalme 59

To the chief musician Altaschith, Michtam of
David: when Saul sent, & they watched the
house to kill him.

O GOD from them deliver mee
    that are mine enemies:
  set thou me up on high from them
    that up against me rise.

2 Deliver mee from them that work
    grievous-iniquity:
  and be a saviour unto mee

                    from

from men that be bloody.

3 For loe,they for my soule lay wayt;
  the strong causlesse combine
against me,not for my crime,Lord,
  nor any sin of mine.

4 Without iniquity in me
  they run, & ready make
themselves,doe thou behold,also
  unto my help awake.

5 Lord God of hoast,thou Israels God,
  rise to visit therefore
all heathens;who sin wilfully,
  to them shew grace no more.

6 At ev'ning they returne,& like
  to dogs a noyse doe make;
and so about the city round
  a compasse they doe take.

7 Behold they belch out with their mouths,
  within their lips swords are:
for who is he (doe these men say)
  which *us* at all doth heare.

8 But thou o *Lord*,at them wilt laugh,
  and heathens all wilt mock.

9 *And for* his strength. I'le wayt on thee
  for God is my high Rock.
             (2)
10 God of my mercy manyfold
  with good shall prevent mee:
and my desire upon my foes
  the Lord will let mee see.

11 Slay them not,lest my folk forget:

                              but

but scatter them abroad
    by thy strong-power;& bring **them downe,**
who art our shield o God..
12 For their mouths sin,& their lips words,
    and in their pride them take:
and for their cursing,& lying
    which in their speech they make.
13 Consume in wrath, consume & let
    them be no more;that they
may know that God in Iacob rules,
    to th'ends of th'earth. Selah.
14 And at ev'ning let them returne,
    and like dogs a noyse make;
and so about the citty round
    a compasse let them take.
15 And let them wander up & downe
    seeking what they may eat,
and if they be not satisfiyde,
    then let them grudge thereat,
16 But I will sing thy powre;& shout
    i'th morning thy kindenesse:
for thou my towre & refuge art
    in day of my distresse.
17 Thou art my strength,& unto thee,
    sing psalmes of prayse will I:
for God is mine high towre, he is
    the God of my mercy.

Psalme 60.

To the chief musician upon Shushan Eduth
Michtam of David,to teach. when he strove with
Aram Naharaim, & with Aram Zobah when
                    Ioab

PSALME lx.

O GOD, thou hast rejected us,
   and scattered us abroad:
thou hast displeased been with us,
   returne to us o God.

2 The land to tremble thou hast caus'd,
   thou it asunder brake:
doe thou the breaches of it heale,
   for it doth moveing shake.

3 Thou hast unto thy people shew'd
   things that are hard, thou hast
also the cup of trembleing
   given to them to tast.

4 But unto them that doe thee feare,
   a Banner to display
thou given hast to be lift up
   for thy truths sake. Selah.

5 That those who thy beloved are
   delivered may bee,
o doe thou save with thy right hand,
   and answer give to mee.

6 God in his holynes hath spoke,
   rejoyce therein will I,
Shechem I will divide, & meete
   of Succoth the valley.

7 To mee doth Gilead appertaine,
   Manasseh mine besides:
Ephraim the strength is of my head,
   Iudah my lawes prescribes.

8 Moab's my wash-pot, I will cast

O   over

over Edom my ſhoo,
  o Paleſtine, becauſe of mee
  be thou triumphant too.
9 O who is it that will mee lead
    to th'citty fortifyde?
  and who is he that will become
    into Edom my guide?
10 Is it not thou, o God, who hadſt
    caſt us off heretofore?
  and thou o God, who with our hoaſts
    wouldſt not goe out before?
11 O give to us help from diſtreſſe
    for mans help is but vaine:
12 Through God wee'l doe great acts, he ſhall
    our foes tread with diſdaine.

Pſalme 61

To the chief muſician upon Neginath,
  A pſalme of David.

HArken o God, unto my cry,
  unto my prayr attend.
2 When my heart is oppreſt, I'le cry
    to thee from the earths end.
  Doe thou mee lead unto the rock
    that higher is then I.
3 For thou my hiding-place, haſt been
    ſtrong Fort from th'enemy.
4 Within thy Tabernacle I
    for ever will abide,
  within the covert of thy wings
    I'le ſeek my ſelfe to hide.   Selah·
5 For thou o God, haſt heard the vowes

                                    that

that I to thee have paſt:
their heritage that feare thy name
to mee thou given haſt.

6 Thou to the dayes of the Kings life
   wilt make addition:
his yeares as generation,
   and generation.

7 Before the face of the ſtrong God
   he ſhall abide for aye:
doe thou mercy & truth prepare
   that him preſerve they may.

8 So then I will unto thy name
   ſing prayſe perpetually,
that I the vowes which I have made
   may pay continually.

Pſalme 62

To the chief muſician, to Ieduthun,
   a pſalme of David.

TRuly my ſoule in ſilence waytes
   the mighty God upon:
from him it is that there doth come
   all my ſalvation.

2 He only is my rock, & my
   ſalvation; it is hee
that my defence is, ſo that I
   mov'd greatly ſhall not bee.

3 How long will yee miſchief deviſe
   'gainſt man; be ſlaine yee ſhall,
all yee are as a rottring fence,
   & like a bowing wall.

4 Yet they conſult to caſt him downe

O 2

from

from his excellency:
lyes they doe love,with mouth they blesse,
 but they curse inwardly.   Selah.
5 Yet thou my soule in silent wayt
 the mighty God upon:
because from him there doth arise
 my expectation.
6 He only is my rock,& my
 salvation; it is hee
that my defence is, so that I
 shall never mooved bee.
7 In God is my salvation,
 also is my glory:
and the rock of my fortitude,
 my hope in God doth ly.
8 Yee people,see that you on him
 doe put your trust alway,
before him poure ye out your hearts:
 God is our hopefull-stay.   Selah.
9 Surely meane men are vanity
 high mens sonnes are a lye:
in ballance laid together are
 lighter then vanity.
10 In robbery be not vaine,trust not
 yee in oppression:
if so be riches doe increase
 set not your heart *thereon*.
11 The mighty God hath spoken once:
 once & againe this word
I have it heard that *all* power
 belongs unto the Lord.

12 Also

12 Also to thee benignity
   o Lord, doth *appertaine*:
for thou according to his work
   rendrest each man againe.

Psalme 63

A psalme of David, when he was in the
wildernes of Iudah.

O GOD, thou art my God, early
   I will for thee inquire:
my soule thirsteth for thee, my flesh
   for thee hath strong desire,
In land whereas no water is
   that thirsty is & dry.

2 To see, as I saw in thine house
   thy strength & thy glory.

3 Because thy loving kindenes doth
   abundantly excell
ev'n life it selfe: wherefore my lips
   forth shall thy prayses tell.

4 Thus will I blessing give to thee
   whilst that alive am I:
and in thy name I will lift up
   these hands of mine on high.

5 My soule as with marrow & fat
   shall satisfied bee:
my mouth also with joyfull lips
   shall prayse give unto thee.

6 When as that I remembrance have
   of thee my bed upon,
and on thee in the night watches
   have meditation.

O 3

7 Be

7 Becauſe that thou haſt been to me
  he that to me help brings;
 therefore will I ſing joyfully
  in ſhaddow of thy wings.

8 My ſoule out of an ardent love
  doth follow after thee:
 alſo thy right hand it is that
  which hath upholden mee.

9 But as for thoſe that ſeek my ſoule
  to bring it to an end,
 they ſhall into the lower parts
  of the earth downe deſcend.

10 By the hand of the ſword alſo
  they ſhall be made to fall:
 and they be for a portion
  unto the Foxes ſhall.

11 But the King ſhall rejoyce in **God**,
  all that by him doe ſweare
 ſhall glory, but ſtopped ſhall be
  their mouths that lyars are.

Pſalme 64
To the chief muſician, a pſalme
of David.

O GOD, when I my prayer make,
  my voyce *then* doe thou heare;
 alſo doe thou preſerve my life
  ſafe from the enemies feare.

2 And from the ſecret counſell of
  the wicked hide thou mee:
 from th' inſurection of them
  that work iniquitee.

3 who

3 Who have their tongue now sharpened
  like as it were a sword;
and bend *their bowes to shoot* their shafts
  ev'n a most bitter word:

4 That they in secrecie may shoot
  the perfect man to hitt.
suddenly doe they shoot at him,
  & never feare a whitt.

5 Them selves they in a matter ill
  encourage; how they may
lay snares in secret, thus they talk;
  who shall them see? they say.

6 They doe search out iniquity,
  a search exact they keep:
both inward thought of euery man
  also the heart is deep.

7 But God shall shoot at them a shaft,
  be sudden their wound shall.

8 So that they shall make their owne tongue
  upon themeslves to fall,
All that see them shall flee away.

9 All men shall feare, & tell
the works of God, for his doeing
  they shall consider well.

10 The just shall in the Lord be glad,
  and trust in him he shall:
and they that upright are in heart
  in him shall glory all.

Psalme 65
To the chief musician, a psalme and
  song of David.

I SALM

O GOD, in Sion silently
 prayse wayteth upon thee:
and thankfully unto thee shall
 the vow performed bee.

2 O thou that harken dost unto
 the prayr that men doe make,
ev'n unto thee therefore all flesh
 themselves they shall betake.

3 Works of iniquitie they have
 prevailed against mee;
as for our trespasses they shall
 be purgde away by thee.

4 O blessed is the man of whom
 thou thy free choyce dost make;
and that he may dwell in thy courts
 him neere to thee dost take:
For with the good things of thy house
 be satisfyde shall wee;
and with the holy things likwise
 that in thy temple bee.

5 In righteousnes, thou, by the things
 that dreadfully are done,
wilt answer give to us, o God,
 of our salvation:
Vpon whom all the ends of th'earth
 do confidently stay,
& likewise they that are remov'd
 far off upon the sea.

6 He sets fast mountaines by his strength
7 girt with might. Hee doth swage
 the noyse of seas, noyse of their waves

also

also the peoples rage.

(2)

8 They at thy tokens are afrayd
    that dwell in parts far out;
out goings of the morning thou
    and ev'ning makst to shout.

9 Thou visitest the earth,& dost
    it moisten plenteously,
thou with Gods streame,full of water
    enrichest it greatly:
When thou hast so prepared it,
    thou dost them corne prepare.

10 The ridges thou abundantly
    watrest that in it are;
The furrows of it thou setlest,
    with showers that do fall
thou makst it soft,thou dost therof
    the springing blesse withall.

11 Thou dost the yeare with thy goodnes
    adorne as with a crowne,
also the paths where thou dost tread,
    fatnes they doe drop downe.

12 They drop upon the pastures that
    are in the wildernes;
and girded are the little hills
    about with joyfullnes.

13 Clothed the pastures are with flocks,
    corne over-covering
the valleys is;so that for joy
    they shout, they also sing.

P

Pſalme 66

To the chief muſician a pſalme or ſong.

O All yee lands, a joyfull noyſe
 unto God doe yee rayſe.

2 Sing forth the honour of his name:
  make glorious his prayſe.

3 How dreadfull in thy works art thou?
  unto the Lord ſay yee:
  through thy powres greatnes thy foes ſhall
  ſubmit themſelves to thee.

4 All they ſhall bow themſelves to thee
  that dwell upon the earth,
  and ſing unto thee, they ſhall ſing
  unto thy name with mirth.   Selah.

5 Come hither, alſo of the works
  of God take yee notice,
  he in his doing terrible
  towards mens children is.

6 He did the ſea into dry land
  convert, a way they had
  on foot to paſſe the river through,
  there we in him were glad.

7 He ruleth by his powre for ever,
  his eyes the nations ſpie:
  let not thoſe that rebellious are
  lift up themſelves on high.   Selah.

8 Yee people bleſſe our God,& make (2 part)
  his prayſes voyce be heard.

9 Which holds our ſoule in life, our feet
  nor ſuffers to be ſtird.

10 For God thou haſt us prov'd, thou haſt

                                          us

us tryde as silver's tryde.

11 Into the net brought us,thou haft
on our loynes ftreightnes tyde.

12 Men o're our heads thou madft to ride,
through fire & water paffe
did wee,but us thou broughft into
a place that wealthy was.

13 With offrings I'le go to thine houfe:
my vowes I'le pay to thee.

14 Which my lips uttred, & mouth fpake,
when trouble was on mee.

15 Burnt offrings I'le offer to thee
that full of fatnes are,
with the incenfe of rams,I will
bullocks with goates prepare.   Selah.

16 Come harken unto me all yee   (3 part)
of God that fearers are,
and what he hath done for my foule
to you I will declare.

17 With mouth I cryde to him, & with
my tongue extoll'd was hee.

18 If in my heart I fin regard
the Lord will not heare mee.

19 But God that is moft mighty hath
me heard affuredly;
unto the voyce of my prayr he
lift'ned-attentively.

20 Bleft be the mighty God,becaufe
neither my prayr hath hee,
nor yet his owne benignity,
turned away from mee.

Pſalme 67

To the chief muſician on Neginoth
a pſalme *or* Song.

GOD gracious be to us,& give
his bleſſing us unto,
let him upon us make to ſhine
his countenance alſo.   Selah.

2 That there may be the knowledg of
thy way the earth upon,
and alſo of thy ſaving health
in every nation.

3 O God let thee the people prayſe,
let all people prayſe thee.

4 O let the nations rejoyce,
and let them joyfull bee:
For thou ſhalt give judgement unto
the people righteouſly,
alſo the nations upon earth
thou ſhalt them lead ſafely.   Selah.

5 O God let thee the people prayſe
let all people prayſe thee.

6 *Her* fruitfull increaſe by the earth
ſhall then forth yeilded bee:
God ev'n our owne God ſhall us bleſſe.

7 God *I ſay* bleſſe us ſhall,
and of the earth the utmoſt coaſts
they ſhall him reverence all.

Pſalme 68

To the chief muſician,a pſalme or ſong
of David.

pſalme

Let God arise, his enemies
  let them disperfed bee,
let them alfo that doe him hate
  away from his face flee.

2 As fmoake is driven away, ev'n fo
  doe thou them drive away:
as wax at fire melts, in Gods fight
  let wicked fo decay.

3 But let the righteous ones be glad:
  o let them joyfull bee
before the Lord, alfo let them
  rejoyce exceedinglie.

4 Sing to God, to his name fing prayfe,
  extoll him that doth ride
on fkies, by his name IAH, before
  his face joyfull abide.

5 A father of the fatherleffe,
  and of the widdows cafe
God is a judge, & that within
  his holy dwelling place.

6 God feates the defolate in houfe,
  brings forth thofe that are bound
in chaines, but the rebellious
  dwell in a barren ground.

(2)

7 O God when as thou didft goe forth
  in prefence of thy folk,
when through the defart wildernes
  thou diddeft marching walk.   Selah.

8 The earth did at Gods prefence fhake,
  from heav'ns the drops downe fell:

P 3   Sinai

Sinai it selfe moved before
the God of Israell.

9 O God thou on thy heritage
  didst send a plenteous raine,
whereby when as it weary was
  thou it confirm'd againe.

10 Thy congregation hath dwelt
  therin, thou dost prepare
  o God of thy goodnes, for them
  that poore afflicted are.

11 The Lord the word gave, great their troup
  that it have published.

12 Kings of hoasts fled, fled, she that stayd
  at home spoyle devided.

13 Though yee have lyen among the pots,
  be like doves wings shall yee
with silver deckt, & her feathers
  like yellow gold that bee.

14 When there th'Almighty scattred Kings,
  t'was white as Salmons snow.

15 Gods hill like Bashan hill, high hill,
  like Bashan hill unto.

16 Why doe ye leap ye lofty hills?
  this is the very hill
in which God loves to dwell, the Lord
  dwell in it ever will.

(3)

17 Gods charrets twice ten thousand fold,
  thousands of Angells bee;
with them as in his holy place,
  on Sinai mount is hee.

18 Thou didst ascend on high, thou ledst
  captivity captive,
                                    for

for men, yea, for rebells also
  thou diddest gifts receive;
That the Lord God might dwell with them.
19 Who dayly doth us load
  with benefits, blest be the Lord
    that's our salvations God.   Selah.
20 He is God of salvation
    that is our God most strong:
  and unto Iehovah the Lord
    issues from death belong.
21 But God shall wound the enemies head,
    the hairy scalp also
  of him that in his trespasses
    on forward still doth go.
(4)
22 The Lord sayd I'le bring back againe,
    againe from Bashan hill:
  my people from the depths of seas
    bring back againe I will.
23 That thy foot may be dipt within
    blood of thine enemyes;
  imbrude the tongue of thy dogs may
    be in the same likewyse.
24 They have thy goings seene o God
    thy goings in progresse;
  ev'n of my God my King within
    place of his holynesse.
25 Singers went first, musicians then,
    in midst maids with Timbrel.
26 Blesse God i'th Churches, the Lord from
    the spring of Israell.
27 There litle Benjamin the chief
    with Iudahs Lords, & their   counsel

PSALM lxviii.

counsell, with Zebulons princes,
    and Naphtalies lords were.
23 That valliant strength the which thou hast
    thy God hath commanded,
strengthen o God, the thing which thou
    for us hast effected.

(4)

29 For thy house at Ierusalem
    Kings shall bring gifts to thee.
30 Rebuke the troups of spearmen, troups
    of bulls that mighty bee:
With peoples calves, with him that stoops
    with peeces of silvar:
o scatter thou the people that
    delight themselves in war.
31 Princes shall out of Egipt come,
    & Ethiopias land
shall speedily unto the Lord
    reach her out-streched hand.
32 Earths kingdomes sing yee unto God:
    unto the Lord sing prayse.   Selah.
33 To him that rides on heav'ns of heav'ns
    that were of ancient dayes:
Loe, he his voyce, a strong voyce gives.
34   To God ascribe yee might,
his excellence o're Israell is,
    & his strength in the height.
35 God fearfull from his holy place
    the God of Israell, hee
gives strength & powre unto his folk,
    o let God blessed bee.

psalme

PSALME lxix.

To the chief mufician upon Shofhannim,
A pfalme of David.

THe waters in unto my foule
   are come, o God, me fave.
2 I am in muddy deep funk downe,
   where I no ftanding have:
Into deep waters I am come,
   where floods mee overflow.
3 I of my crying weary am,
   my throat is dryed fo;
Mine eyes faile: I wayt for my God.
4   They that have hated mee
without a caufe, then mine heads haires
   they more in number bee:
Alfo mine enemies wrongfully
   they are that would me flay,
mighty they are; then I reftor'd
   what I took not away.
5 O God thou knowft my foolifhnes;
   my fin's not hid from thee.
6 Who wayt on thee, Lord God of hoafts,
   let not be fhamd for mee:
O never fuffer them, who doe
   for thee inquiry make,
o God of Ifraell, to be
   confounded for my fake,
(2)
7 By reafon that I for thy fake,
   reproach have fuffered:
confufion my countenance
   hath overcovered.

Q

8 I as a stranger am become
 unto my bretherren;
and am an aliant unto
 my mothers childerren.

9 For of thy house the zeale me hath
 up eaten: every one
who thee reproach, their reproaches
 are fallen mee upon

10 In fasts, I wept & spent my soule,
 this was reproach to mee.

11 And I my garment sackcloth made:
 yet must their proverb bee.

12 They that do sit within the gate,
 against mee speak they do;
unto the drinkers of strong drink,
 I was a song also.

13 But I in an accepted time
 to thee Lord, make my prayr:
mee Lord, in thy salvations truth,
 in thy great mercy heare.

(3)

14 Deliver me out of the mire,
 and mee from sinking keep:
let mee be freed mine haters from,
 and out of waters deep.

15 O'reflow mee let not water floods,
 nor mee let swallow up
the deep, also let not the pitt
 her mouth upon mee shut.

16 Iehovah heare thou mee, for good
 is thy benignity:

turne

turne unto mee according to
   greatnes of thy mercy.
17 And hide not thou thy countenance
   from thy servant away;
because that I in trouble am;
   heare me without delay.
18 O draw thou nigh unto my soule,
   doe thou it vindicate;
give mee deliverance, because
   of them that doe mee hate.
19 Thou hast knowne my reproach, also
   my shame, & my disgrace:
mine adversaryes every one
   they are before thy face.

(4)

20 Reproach mine heart brake, I was griev'd:
   for some me to bemone
I sought, but none there was; & for
   comforters, but found none.
21 Moreover in stead of my meate
   unto mee gall they gave;
and in me thirst they vineger
   for drink made me to have.
22 Their table set before their face,
   to them become a snare:
and *that let be* a trap, *which should
have been* for *their* welfare.
23 And let their eyes be darkened,
   that they may never see:
their loynes also with trembleing
   to shake continuallee.

Q 2   24 Poure

24 Poure out thine ire on them, let seize
    on them thine anger fell.

25 Their Pallace let be desolate:
    none in their tents let dwell.

26 Because they *him* doe persecute
    on whom thy stroke is found:
   also they talk unto the grief
    of them whom thou dost wound.

27 Thou unto their iniquity
    iniquity doe add:
   into thy righteousnes for them
    let entrance none be had.

28 Out of the book of the living
    o doe thou them forth blot,
   and amongst them that righteous are
    be written let them not.

(5)

29 But Lord, I'me poore & sorrowfull:
    let thy health lift me hy.

30 With song I'le prayse the name of God:
    with thanks him magnify.

31 Vnto Iehovah*this* also
    shall be more pleasing far,
   then *any* oxe *or* bullock young,
    that horn'd & hoofed are.

32 This thing when as they shall behold,
    then shall be glad the meek;
   also their heart shall ever live
    that after God doe seek.

33 For the Lord hears the poore, nor doth
    despise whom he hath bound.

34 Let heav'n, earth, seas & all therin
   that moves, his prayses sound.
35 For God will Iudahs cittyes build,
   and Sion he will save:
   that they may dwell therin, & may
   it in possession have.
36 The seed also of his servants
   inherit shall the same:
   also therin inhabit shall
   they that doe love his name.

Psalme 70

To the chief musician, a psalme to bring
to remembrance.

O GOD, to rescue mee,
   Lord, to mine help, make hast.
2 Let them that after my soule seek
   asham'd be, & abasht:
   Turnd back & shamd let them
   that in my hurt delight.
3 Turnd back let them ha, ha, that say,
   their shame for to requite.
4 Let all those that thee seek
   joy, & be glad in thee:
   let such as love thy health say still,
   magnifyde let God bee.
5 Make hast to me Lord, for
   I poore am & needy:
   thou art mine ayd, & my helper
   o Lord, doe not tarry.

Psalme 71

PSALM lxx1.

IEHOVAH, I for safety doe
  betake my selfe to thee:
    o let me not at any time
      put to confusion bee.

2 Me rescue in thy righteousnes,
    let me deliverance have:
  to me doe thou incline thine eare,
    also doe thou me save.

3 Be thou my dwelling Rock, whereto
    I alwayes may resort:
  thou gav'st commandment me to save,
    for thou my Rock & Fort.

4 Out of the hand of the wicked
    my God, deliver mee,
  out of the hand of the unjust,
    leaven'd with crueltie.

5 For thou o God, Iehovah art
    mine expectation:
  and thou art hee whom from my youth
    my trust is set upon :

6 Thou hast upheld mee from the womb,
    thou art he that tookst mee
  out of my mothers belly; still
    my prayse shall be of thee.

(2)

7 To many I a wonder am
    but thou my refuge strong.

8 Let my mouth fill'd be with thy prayse,
    & honour all day long .

9 Within the time of elder age
    o cast me not away,

                        and

and doe not thou abandon me
 when my ftrength doth decay.
10 Becaufe they that be enemyes
 to me, againft me fpake,
and they that for my foule lay-wayt,
 counfell together take.
11 Saying, God hath forgotten him:
 doe yee him now purfue,
and apprehend him, for *there is*
 not one him to refcue.
12 Depart not farre from mee, o God,
 my God haft to helpe mee.
13 The adverfaryes of my foule,
 let them afhamed bee:
Let them confumed be, let them
 be alfo covered,
both with reproach & difhonour,
 that for my hurt wayted.
   (3)
14 But *I* with patience will wayt
 on thee continuallee,
and I will adde yet more & more
 to all the prayfe of thee.
15 My mouth it fhall thy righteoufnes,
 and thy falvation fhow
from day to day, for *of the fame*
 no number doe I know.
16 In the ftrong might of God the Lord
 goe on a long will I:
I'le mention make of thy juftice,
 yea ev'n of thine only.

17 From my youth up o mighty God,
     thou hast instructed mee:
and hitherto I have declar'd
     the wonders wrought by thee.

18 And now unto mine elder age,
     and hoary head, o God,
doe not forsake mee: till I have
     thy power showne abroad,
Vnto this generation,
     and unto every one
that shall hereafter be to come,
     thy strong dominion.

(4)

19 Thy righteousnes o God, it doth
     reach up on high also,
great are the things which thou hast done;
     Lord who's like thee unto?

20 Thou who hast caused mee to see
     afflictions great & sore,
shalt mee revive, & me againe
     from depths of earth restore.

21 Thou shalt my greatnes multiply
     & comfort me alwayes.

22 Also with tuned *P*saltery
     I will shew forth thy prayse,
O thou my God, I will sing forth
     to thee mine Harp upon,
thy verity & faithfullnes,
     o Israels Holy-one.

23 My lips with shouting shall rejoyce
     when I shall sing to thee:

my

my soule also, which freely thou
   haſt brought to liberty.
24 Likewiſe my tongue ſhall utter forth
   thy juſtice all day long:
for they confounded are, & brought
   to ſhame, that ſeek my wrong.

Pſalme 72

A psalme for Solomon.

O GOD, thy judgements give the King,
   & thy juſtice to the Kings Sonne.
2 He ſhall thy folk with juſtice judge,
   & to thy poore ſee judgement done,
3   The mountaines ſhall abundantly
unto the people bring forth peace:
the little hills ſhall bring the ſame,
by executing righteouſnes.
4   Poore of the people he ſhall judge,
and children of the needy ſave;
& he in peeces ſhall break downe
each one that them oppreſſed have.
5   They ſhall thee feare, while Sun & moon
endure through generations all.
6 Like raine on mowne graſſe he ſhall come:
as ſhowres on earth diſtilling-fall.
7   The juſt ſhall flouriſh in his dayes,
& ſtore of peace till no moone bee.
8 And from the ſea unto the ſea,
from floud to lands end reigne ſhall hee.
9   They that within the wildernes
doe dwell, before him bow they muſt:
and they who are his enemies

they verily shall lick the dust.

(2)

10 Vpon him presents shall bestow
of Tarshish, & the Iles, the Kings,
Shebahs, & Sebahs Kings also,
shall unto him give offerings.

11 Yea to him all the kings shall fall,
& serve him every nation:

12 For needy crying save he shall,
the poore, & helper that hath none.

13 The poore & needy he shall spare,
and the soules of the needy save.

14 Their soules from fraud & violence
by him shall free redemption have:
And pretious in his sight shall be

15 the bloud of them. And he shall live,
and unto him shall *every one*
of purest gold of Shebah give:
Also each one their humble prayr
in his behalfe shall make alwayes:
and every one his blessednes
shall dayly celebrate with prayse.

(3)

16 Of corne an handfull there shall be
ith land the mountains tops upon,
the fruit whereof shall moving shake
like to the trees of Lebanon:
And they that of the citty be
like grasse on earth shall flourish all.

17 His name for ever shall indure
as long as Sun continue shall:

PSALME lxxii.

So shall his name continued be,
and men in him themselves shall blesse,
and all the nations of the world
shall him the blessed one professe.

18 O let Iehovah blessed be,
the God, the God of Israell,
hee worketh by himselfe alone
such things whereat men may marvell.

19 And blessed be his glorious name
for ever, let the whole earth be
fill'd full with glory of the same,
Amen, also Amen *say wee.*

This.   *After the common tunes.*

19 And aye be blest his glorious name,
    also let the earth all
be filled with his glorious fame,
    Amen, & so it shall.

---

20   The prayers of David, the
        Son of Iesse, are
            ended.

THIRD BOOKE.

Pſalme 73
A pſalme of Aſaph.

TRuly to Iſraell God is good;
    to men of a cleane heart.

2 But my feet almoſt ſlipt, my ſteps
    aſide did well nigh ſtart.

3 For I was envious at the fooles,
    in peace to ſee the ill.

4 For in their death no band's there are,
    but firme their ſtrength is ſtill.

5 Like other meane men they are not
    in toyleſome miſery,
nor are they ſtricken with like plagues
    as other mortals bee.

6 Therefore doth pride like to a chaine
    encompaſſe them about,
and like a garment; violence
    doth cover them throughout.

7 Within the fatnes *which they have*
    extended are their eyes:
greater proſperity they have
    then their hearts can deviſe.

8 Corrupt they are, & wickedly
    ſpeak guile: proudly they talk.

9 Againſt the heav'ns they ſet their mouth;
    their tongue through th'earth doth walk.

10 There-

(2)

10 Therefore his people unto them
     have hither turned in,
 and waters out of a full cup
     wrung out to them have been.

11 And they have sayd, how can it be
     that God this thing should know,
 & is there in the highest one
     knowledge hereof also?

12 Loe, these are the ungodly ones
     who have tranquillity:
 within the world they doe increase
     in rich ability.

13 Surely in vaine in purity
     cleansed my heart have I.

14 And hands in innocence have washt,
     for plagu'd am I dayly:
 And every morning chastened.

15   If I think thus to say,
   thy childrens generation
     loe then I should betray;

16 And when this poynt to understand
     casting I did devise,
 the matter too laborious
     appeared in mine eyes.

17 Vntill unto the sanctuary
     of God I went, & then
 I prudently did understand
     the last end of these men.

(1)

18 Surely in places slippery

these men thou placed hast:
and into desolations
   thou dost them downward cast.

19 As in a moment, how are they
   brought to destruction?
how are they utterly consum'd
   with sad confusion?

20 Like to a dreame when as a man
   awaking doth arise,
so thou o God, when thou awakst
   their Image shalt despise.

21 My heart thus was leaven'd with grief,
   prickt were my reins by mee:

22 So foolish was I, & knew not,
   like a beast before thee.

(4)

23 Neverthelesse continually
   before thee I doe stand:
thou hast upheld mee stedfastly
   also by my right hand.

24 Thou with thy prudent counsell shalt
   guidance unto mee give:
up afterward also thou shalt
   to glory mee receive.

25 In heavn above but thee alone
   who is it that I have?
and there is nothing upon earth
   besides thee that I crave.

25 This flesh of mine, my heart also
   doth faile me altogether:
but God the strength is of my heart,

and

and portion mine for ever.

27 For loe, they that are far from thee
utterly perish shall:
those who a whoring goe from thee
thou hast destroyed all.

23 But as for mee, for mee it's good
neere God for to repaire:
in God the Lord I put my trust,
all thy works to declare.

Psalme 74
Maschil of Asaph.

O GOD, why hast thou cast us off,
why doth thy rage indure?
for ever smoaking out against
the sheep of thy pasture?

2 Thy congregation call to minde
of old by thee purchast:
the rod of thine inheritance
which thou redeemed hast,
This mount Sion wherin thou dwelst.

3 Lift up thy foot on hye,
unto the desolations
of perpetuity:
Thy foe within the Sanctuary
hath done all lewd designes.

4 Amidst thy Church thy foes doe roare:
their Banners set for signes.

5 The man that axes on thick trees
did lift up had renowne:

6 But now with axe & maules at once,
her carv'd works they beat downe.

7 Thy

7 Thy sanctuaryes into fire
    they cast, the dwelling place
of thy name downe unto the ground
    prophanely they did raze.
8 Let us together them destroy,
    thus in their hearts they sayd:
Gods Synagogues throughout the land
    all in the flames they layd.
        (?)
9 Our signes we see not, there's no more
    a Prophet us among:
nor with us any to be found
    that understands how long.
10 How long shall the oppressing foe
    o mighty God, defame?
thine enemy for evermore
    shall he blaspheme thy name?
11 Why dost thou thus withdraw thine hand,
    the right hand of thy strength?
out of thy bosom o doe thou
    draw it forth to the length.
12 Because the mighty God hath been
    from ancient time my King,
in middest of the earth he is
    salvation working.
13 Thou diddest by thy mighty powre
    devide the sea asunder:
the Dragons heads in peeces thou
    didst break the waters under.
14 The heads of the Leviathan
    thou into peeces brake:

to people that in desarts dwell
    for meat thou didst him make.
15 Thou clav'st the fountain & the floud,
    thou dri'dst up flouds of might.
16 Thine is the day, & night is thine:
    thou Sun prepar'st, & light.
17 Thou all the borders of the earth
    hast constituted fast :
the summer & the winter cold
    the same thou formed hast.

(⅓)

18 Remember this, the enemy
    reproachfully doth blame,
  o Lord, also the foolish folk
    blasphemed have thy name.
19 O doe not to the multitude
    thy turtles soule deliver:
the congregation of thy poore
    forget not thou for ever.
20 Vnto thy cov'nant have respect:
    because the dark places
of th'earth with habitations
    are full of furiousnes.
21 O let not the oppressed one
    returne away with shame:
  o let the poor & needy one
    give prayse unto thy name.
22 Arise o God, plead thine owne cause:
    have thou in memorie
how day by day the foolish man
    with scorne reproacheth thee.

                S   23 Thine

23 Thine enemyes voyce forget not thou:
the loud tumult of thofe
continually on high afcends
that rife thee to oppofe.

Pfalme 75

To the chief mufician Altafchith, pfalme
or fong of Afaph.

O GOD, to thee doe we give thanks,
thanks give we unto thee:
& that thy name is neere at hand;
thy wonders fhew to bee.

2 When I th'affembly fhall receive
uprightly judge I will.

2 Th'earth & its dwellers all do melt:
I ftay its pillars ftill,

4 I did unto the foolifh fay,
deale not fo foolifhly:
alfo unto the wicked ones,
lift not the horne on hye.

5 Lift yee not up your horne on high:
with ftiffned neck fpeak nor,

6 For neither from Eaft, Weft, nor South,
promotion can be got.

7 But God is judge: he fets up one,
another downe doth tread.

8 For in the Lords hand is a cup,
alfo the wine is red:
It's full of mixture, & thereout
he poures: but on earth all
the wicked ones the dregs therof
both ftrein, & drink them fhall.

9 But as for me I will declare,

for evermore I will
sing prayses unto him that is
the God of Iacob *still*.

10 Of men ungodly all the hornes
also cut off will I:
but the hornes of the righteous,
shall be exalted high.

Psalme 76

To the chief musician, on Neginoth, a psalm
or song of Asaph

IN Iudah God is knowne: his name
is great in Israell.

2 In Salem also is his tent:
in Sion he doth dwell,

3 There brake he th'arrows of the bow,
the shield, sword, & battell.   Selah.

4 Illustrious thou art, thou dost
the mounts of prey excell.

5 They that are stout of heart are spoyld,
they slept their sleep profound:
and of the men of might there is
none that their hands have found.

6 Of Iacob o thou mighty God,
as thy rebuke out past,
the chariot also, & the horse
in a dead sleepe are cast.

(2)

7 Thou ev'n thou art to be feared,
and who is it before
thy presence that can stand, when as
that thou art angry sore?

8 Thou diddest cause for to be heard   judge.

judgement from heav'n above:
  the earth exceedingly did feare,
    also it did not move.
9 When as the mighty God arose,
    to th' execution
  of judgement, to save all the meek
    that are the earth upon.   Selah.
10 Assuredly unto thy prayse,
    shall turne the wrath of man:
  & the remainder of the earth
    also thou shalt restraine.
11 Vow, & pay to the Lord your God;
    that him surround all yee,
  and bring ye presents unto him,
    that feared ought to bee.
12 The spirit that in Princes is,
    asunder cut he shall:
  unto the Kings on earth that be,
    dreadfull he is *withall.*

Psalme 77

To the chief musician, to Ieduthun, a
psalme of Asaph.

TO GOD I cryed with my voyce:
    yea with my voyce I have
  cryed unto the mighty God;
    and eare to mee he gave.
2 In my distresse I sought the Lord:
    my sore ran in the night,
  & ceased not: also my soule
    refused comfort quite.
3 I did remember God, also

disqui-

disquieted was I:
I did complaine, & my spirit
o'rewhelmd was heavily.   Selah.

4 Awaking thou dost hold mine eyes:
I cannot speak for feares.

5 I have considered dayes of old,
of ancient times the yeares.

(2)

6 To my remembrance I doe call
the song in night I had:
I commun'd with my heart, also
strict search my spirit made.

7 For ever will the Lord cast off?
& pleasd will he not bee?

8 His tender mercy is it ceast
to perpetuitee?
His promise doth it, faile for aye?

9 Hath God forgot likewise
gracious to be? hath he shut up
in wrath his deare mercyes?   Selah.

10 Then did I say, within my selfe,
tis mine infirmity:
the yeares of the right hand I will
think on of the most high.

(3)

11 I will unto remembrance call
the actions of the Lord:
thy wondrous works of ancient time
surely I will record.

12 I'le muse also of all thy works,
& of thy doings talk.

S 3   13 with-

13 Within the temple is thy way,
 o God, *where thou doſt walk.*
What god ſo great as our God is?
 1 *W*orks wonderfull that are
 thou God haſt done; among the folk
 thou doſt thy ſtrength declare.
15 Thoſe that thy people are thou haſt
 with thine owne arme ſet free,
 of Iacob alſo of Ioſeph
 the childeren that bee. Selah.

(4)
16 Thee did the waters ſee, o God,
 thee did the waters ſee:
 they were afraid, the deeps alſo
 could not but troubled bee.
17 With waters were the clouds pour'd forth,
 the ſkies a ſound out ſent:
 alſo thine arrows on each ſide
 abroad diſperſed went.
18 Thy thunders voyce in heaven was:
 the world illuminate
 thy lightnings did, the earth alſo
 trembled & ſhook hereat.
19 Thy wayes ith ſea, thy paths & ſteps
 unkowne, are in the deep.
20 By Moſes & by Arons hand
 thou ledſt thy folk like ſheep.

Pſalme 78
Maſchil of Aſaph.

Give liſtning eare unto my law,
 yee people that are mine,

unto

unto the sayings of my mouth
doe yee your eare incline.

2 My mouth I'le ope in parables,
    I'le speak hid things of old:

3 Which we have heard & knowne:& which
    our fathers have us told.

4 Them from their children wee'l not hide,
    to th'after age shewing
  the Lords prayses: his strength, & works
    of his wondrous doing.

5 In Iacob he a witnesse set,
    & put in Israell
  a law, which he our fathers charg'd,
    they should their children tell:

6 That th'age to come & children which
    are to be borne might know;
  that they might rise up & the same
    unto their children show.

7 That they upon the mighty God
    their confidence might set:
  and Gods works & his commandment
    might keep & not forget,

8 And might not like their fathers be,
    a stiffe, stout race; a race
  that set not right their hearts: nor firme
    with God their spirit was.

(2)

9 The armed sonnes of Ephraim,
    that went out with their bowe,
  did turne their backs in the day when
    they did to battell goe.

                      10 Gods

10 Gods cov'nant they kept not: to walk
in his law they denyde:
11 His works, & wonders, they forgot,
that he to them defcryde.
12 Things that were mervielous he did
within their fathers fight:
in Egipts land, within the field
of Zoan, *by his might*.
13 He did devide the fea, alfo
he cauf'd them through to paffe:
& he the waters made to ftand
that as an heap it was.
14 With cloud by day, with fire all night
15   he led them; Rocks he clave
in wildernes, as from great deeps
drink unto them he gave.
16 Ev'n from out of the ftony rock
ftreames he did bring alfo,
& caufed water to run downe
like as the rivers do.

(3)

17 Moreover they did adde yet more
againft him for to fin:
by their provoaking the moft high
the wildernes within.
18 And alfo they within their heart
did tempt the God of might:
by afking earneftly for meat
for their foules appetite:
19 Moreover they againft God fpake:
they fayd can God be able

within

within the defart wildernes
    to furnifh us a table:
20 Loe, he the rock fmote, thence gufht out
    waters, & ftreames did flow:
for his folk can he flefh provide,
    can he give bread alfo?
21 The Lord heard, he was wroth for this,
    fo kindled was a fire
'gainft Iacob:&'gainft Ifraell
    there came up wrathfull ire.
22 For they in God believed not:
    nor in his health did hope:
23 Though from above he charg'd the clouds:
    & doores of heav'n fet ope:
        (4)
24 Manna to eate he raind on them;
    & gave them the heavns wheat.
25 Each man of them ate Angells food:
    to th'full he fent them meate.
26 Ith heav'ns he made the Eaft-winde blow:
    brought South-winde by his powre.
27 He flefh on them like duft: wing'd foules
    like the feas fand did fhowre.
28 And in the middeft of their camp
    he caufed it to fall,
ev'n round about on every fide
    their dwelling places *all*.
29 So they did eare, they filled were
    abundantly alfo:
for that which was their owne defire
    he did on them beftow;

      T   30 How-

30 Howbeit they were not estrang'd
   from their lustfull desire:
  but while their meat was in their mouths,

31   Vpon them came Gods ire,
  And slew their fat ones: & smote downe
   of Israell the choise men.

32 Still for all this they sin'd: nor did
   believe his wonders then.

(5)

33 Therefore he did in vanity
   the dayes of their life spend,
  and hastily he brought their yeares
   vnto a fearfull *end*.

34 When he them slew, then after him
   they sought with their desire:
  and they return'd, early also
   did after God enquire.

35 Likewise that God was their strong rock
   they cal'd to memoree:
  and that the mighty God most high,
   was their Redeemer free.

36 Yet with their mouth they flattred him:
   and to him their tongues lyde.

37 For right their heart was not in them:
   nor did in's cov'nant byde.

38 But full of mercy, he forgave
   their sin, & stroyd them not;
  yea, oft he turn'd his wrath aside,
   nor rays'd all's anger hot.

39 For he, that they were but fraile flesh,
   and as it were a winde

that

that paſſeth, & comes not againe,
recalled unto minde.

(6)

40 How oft in deſart vext they him:
and made him there to moane?

41 Yea, they turn'd, tempted God: & did
ſtint Iſr'ells holy one.

42 His hand they did not, nor the day
keep in their remembrance:
wherein he from the enemy
gave them deliverance:

43 And how his ſignes miraculous
in Egipt he had ſhowne:
and his moſt fearfull prodigies
within the field of Zoan:

44 Alſo how he their rivers had
converted into bloud:
& (that they could not drink therof)
the waters of their floud.

45 Amongſt them, which did them devoure,
he ſent forth divers flies:
& them amongſt, which them deſtroyd,
he ſent forth frogs likewiſe.

45 He gave their fruit to th'Caterpillar:
their labour to th'Locuſt.

47 He did their Vines deſtroy with haile:
their Sycamores with froſt.

43 Alſo unto the haile he did
their cattell ſhut up faſt:
likewiſe their heards of cattell to
the fiery thunder blaſt,

T 2   49 He

49 He cast on them fierce ire, & wrath,
    & indignation,
  & sore distresse: by sending forth
    ill Angells them upon.

(7)

50 He made a way unto his wrath,
    and their soule did not save
from death: also their life over
    to Pestilence he gave,

51 He within Egipt land also
    all the first borne did smite:
those that within the tents of Ham
    were chiefest of their might:

52 But he made like a flock of sheep
    his owne folk forth to go:
like to a flock ith wildernes
    he guided them also.

53 And he in safety did them lead
    so that they did not dread:
within the sea their enemies
    he also covered.

54 And to the border he did bring
    them of his holy place:
unto this mountaine which he did
    by his right hand purchase.

55 Fore them he cast the heathen out,
    their lot he did devide
by line: & Isr'ells tribes he made
    in their tents to abide.

(8)

56 Yet they tempted the most high God,

                    and

& griev'd him bitterly:
also his testimonyes they
kept not *attentively* :

57 But like their fathers back they turn'd
and faithlesnesse did show:
they turned were aside ev'n like
to a deceitfull bowe.

58 For they to anger did provoake
him with their places hye:
& with their graven Images,
mov'd him to jealousy.

59 God hearing this, was wroth, & loath'd
Isr'ell with hatred great:

60 So Shilohs tent he left: the tent
which men amongst he set,

61 And he delivered his strength
into captivity:
also into the enemies hand
his beautifull glory.

62 To th'sword he gave his folk: & was
wroth with his heritage.

63 Fire their young men devour'd:their maides
none gave to marriage.

64 Their Priests fell by the sword: also
their widdows did not weepe.

65 Then did the Lord arise as one
awakned out of sleepe:
Like a strong man that after wine

65 doth shout. He also smote
his foes behinde: & so he gave
them an eternall blot.

67 Then he did Iosephs tent refuse:
nor Ephr'ims tribe approv'd.

68 But he the tribe of Iudah chose:
mount Sion which he lov'd.

69 And he his Sanctuary built
like unto places high:
like to the earth which he did found
to perpetuity.

70 Of David also his servant
election he did make,
and from the place of folding up
the sheep he did him take.

71 From following the ewes with young
he did him then advance;
to feed Iacob his folk, also
Isr'ell his heritance.

72 So he according to his hearts
integrity them fed:
and by the wise discretion
of his hands he them led.

Psalme 79
A psalme of Asaph.

O GOD, the heathen entred have
thine heritance, & defylde
thine holy temple: they on heaps
Ierusalem have pylde.

2 The dead bodyes of thy servants
they given have for meate
to th' fowles of heav'n: flesh of thy Saints
for beasts of earth to *eate.*

2 Their

3 Their bloud they have forth powred round
    about Ierusalem
  like unto waters: & there *was*
    none for to bury *them.*

4 To those that neere unto us dwell
    reproach become are wee:
  a scoffing & a scorne to them
    that round about us bee,

5 How long, Iehovah, wilt thou still
    continue in thine ire,
  for ever? shall thy jealousie
    burne like as doth the fire?

6 Vpon the heathen poure thy wrath
    which never did thee know,
  upon the kingdomes that have not
    cal'd on thy name also.

7 Because they Iacob have devour'd:
    his habitation
  they also wondrously have brought
    to desolation.

(2)

8 Minde not against us former sins,
    let thy mercies make hast
  us to prevent: because we are
    neere utterly layd waste.

9 God of our safety, help thou us
    for thy names glory make,
  us free also, & purge away
    our sin for thy names sake.

10 Why say the heathen where's their God?
    with heathen let be knowne

                              before

before our eyes, the vengeance of
   thy servants bloud out flowne.
11 Before thee let the prisoners sighs
   come up, accordingly
as is thy mighty arme: save those
   that are design'd to dye,
12 And to our neighbours seven fold,
   into their bosome pay,
that their reproach, with which o Lord,
   reproached thee have they.
13 So we thy folk & pasture sheepe,
   will give thee thanks alwayes:
and unto generations all,
   wee will shew forth thy prayse.

Psalme 80

To the chief musician upon Shoshannim
   Eduth, a psalme of Asaph.

O Isr'ells shepheard, give thou eare;
   that Ioseph leadst about
like as a flock: that dwelst betweene
   the Cherubims, shine out.
2 Before Ephr'im & Benjamin,
   Manasseh s tribe also,
doe thou stir up thy strength, & come,
   and to us safety show.
3 O God returne thou us againe,
   and cause thy countenance
to shine forth upon us; so wee
   shall have deliverance.
4 Lord God of hoasts, how long wilt thou
   be wroth at thy folks prayrs?

                            thou

5 Thou feedſt with bread of tears, & them
 to drink giv'ſt many teares.

6 A ſtrife unto our neighbours us
 thou doſt alſo expoſe:
and ſcornefully amongſt themſelves
 laugh at us doe our foes.

7 O God of hoaſts, turne us againe,
 & cauſe thy countenance
to ſhine forth upon us, ſo wee
 ſhall have deliverance.

(2)

8 Thou haſt brought out of Egipt land
 a Vine, thou diddeſt caſt
the heathen people forth, alſo
 this *vine* thou planted haſt.

9 Before it thou prepared haſt
 a roome where it might ſtand:
deep root thou didſt cauſe it to take
 and it did fill the land.

10 Her ſhade hid hills, & her boughs did
 like Cedars great *extend*.

11 Her boughs to th'ſea, & her branches
 ſhe to the floud did ſend.

12 Why haſt thou then her hedges made
 quite broken downe to lye,
ſo that all thoſe doe pluck at her
 that in the way paſſe by?

13 The Boare from out the wood he doth
 by waſting it annoy:
& wilde beaſts of the field doe it
 devouringly deſtroy.

V   14 wee

(3)

14 Wee doe beseech thee to returne
o God of hoasts, incline
to look from heaven, & behould,
& visit thou this vine.

15 The vineyard which thou hast also
with thy right hand set fast,
that branch likewise which for thy selfe
strongly confirm'd thou hast.

16 It is consumed with the fire
and utterly cut downe,
perish they doe, & that because
thy countenance doth frowne.

17 Vpon the man of thy right hand
let thine hand present bee:
upon the son of man whom thou
hast made so strong for thee

18 So then from henceforth wee will not
from thee goe back at all:
o doe thou quicken us, & wee
upon thy name will call.

19 Lord God of hoasts, turne us againe,
and cause thy countenance
to shine forth upon us, so wee
shall have deliverance.

Psalme 81

To the chiefe musician upon Gittith,
a psalme of Asaph.

SIng unto God who is our strength,
and that with a loud voyce:
unto him that is Iacobs God

make

make yee a joyfull noyse.

2 Take up a psalme of melodie,
    and bring the Timbrel hither:
the Harp *which soundes* so pleasantly
    with Psaltery together.

3 As in the time of the new moone
    with Trumpet sound on high:
in the appoynted time & day
    of our solemnity.

4 Because that unto Israell
    this thing a statute was;
and by the God of Iacob this
    did for a judgement pass.

5 This witnesse he in Ioseph set
    when as through Egipt land
he went: I there a language heard
    I did not understand.

6 I from the burden which he bare
    his shoulder did set free:
his hands also were from the pots
    delivered by mee.

(2)

7 Thou cal'dst in streights, & I thee freed:
    in thunders secret way
I answred thee, I prov'd thee at
    waters of Meribah.   Selah.

8 Heare o my people, & I will
    testifie unto thee:
o Israell, if that thou wilt
    attention give to mee.

9 Any strange god there shall not be

in

in midst of thee at all:
nor unto any forrein god
   thou bowing downe shalt fall.
10 I am the Lord thy God who thee
   from land of Egipt led:
thy mouth ope wide, & thou by mee
   with plenty shalt be fed.
11 My people yet would not give eare
   unto the voyce I spake:
and Israell would not in mee
   quiet contentment take.
12 So in the hardnes of their heart
   I did them send away,
in their owne consultations
   likewise *then* walked they.

(3)

13 O that my people unto mee
   obedient had bin:
and o that Israell he had
   walked my wayes within.
14 I should within a little time
   have pulled downe their foes:
I should have turn'd my hand upon
   such as did them oppose.
15 The haters of the Lord to him
   obedience should have faynd:
but unto perpetuity
   their time should have remaind.
16 And with the finest of the wheat
   have nourisht them should hee:
with honie of the rock I should

have

have satiſſied thee.

Pſalme 82

A pſalme of Aſaph.

THe mighty God doth ſtand within
    th'aſſemblie of the ſtrong:
    and he it is that righteouſly
    doth judge the gods among.

2 How long a time is it that yee
    will judge unrighteouſlie?
    & will accept the countenance
    of thoſe that wicked bee?

3 See that yee doe defend the poore,
    alſo the fatherleſſe:
    unto the needy juſtice doe,
    and that are in diſtreſſe.

4 The waſted poore, & thoſe that are
    needy deliver yee;
    and them redeeme out of the hand
    of ſuch as wicked bee.

5 They know not, nor will underſtand,
    in darknes they walk on:
    all the foundations of the earth
    quite out of courſe are gone.

6 I ſayd that yee are gods, & ſonnes
    of th'higheſt yee are all.

7 But yee ſhall dye like men, & like
    one of the princes fall.

8 That thou mayſt judge the earth o God,
    doe thou thy ſelfe advance;
    for thou ſhalt have the nations
    for thine inheritance.

PSALM

Pſalme 83

A pſalme or ſong of Aſaph,

O GOD, doe not thou ſilence keep:
o doe not thou refraine
thy ſelfe from ſpeaking, & o God.
doe not thou dumb remaine.

2 For loe, thine enemies that be
doe rage tumultuouſly:
& they that haters be of thee
have lift the head on hye.

3 Againſt thoſe that thy people be
they crafty counſell take;
alſo againſt thy hidden ones
they conſultation make.

4 They ſayd, leſt they a nation be,
let's cut them downe therefore,
that in remembrance Iſr'elſs name
may not be any more.

5 For they together taken have
counſell with one conſent,
and in confederation
againſt thee they are bent.

6 The tabernacles of Edom
and of the Iſhmaelites:
the people of the Haggarens
& of the Moabites.

7 The men of Gebal, with Ammon,
and Amaleck conſpire,
the Philiſtims, with them that be
inhabitants of Tyre.

8 Aſſyria morover is

con-

conjoyned unto them:
& help they have administred
unto Lots childerren.

(2)

9 As thou didst to the Middianites,
so to them be it done:
as unto Sisera & Iabin
at the Brook of Kison

10 Who neere to Endor suddenly
were quite discomfited:
who also did become as dung
that on the earth is *spred*.

11 Like unto Oreb, & like Zeeb
make thou their Nobles fall,
yea, as Zeba & Zalmunna
make thou their Princes all.

12 Who sayd, for our possession
Gods houses let us take.

13 My God, thou like a wheel, like straw
before the winde them make.

14 As fire doth burne a wood, & as
the flame sets hills on fire:

15 So with thy tempest them pursue,
& fright them in thine ire.

16 Doe thou their faces all fill full
of ignominious shame:
that so they may o Lord, be made
to seek after thy name.

17 Confounded let them ever be,
and terrible troubled:
yea, let them be put unto shame,

and bee extinguished.

18 That men may know; that thou whose name
IEHOVAH is only,
art over all the earth throughout
advanced the most high.

Psalme 84

To the chief musician upon Gittith a psalm
for the sonnes of Korah.

HOw amiable Lord of hoasts
thy tabernacles bee?

2 My soule longs for Iehovahs courts,
yea it ev'n faints in mee.
Mine heart, my flesh also cryes out
after the living God:

3 Yea ev'n the sparrow hath found out
an house *for hir aboad.*
Also the swallow *findes* her nest
thine Altars *neere unto*
where shee her young layes: Lord of hoasts,
my King, my God also.

4 Blest they that dwell within thy house:
still they will give thee prayse.   Selah.

5 Blest is the man whose strength's in thee,
in whose heart are their wayes.

6 Who as they passe through Baca's Vale
doe make it a fountaine:
also the pooles *that are therin*
are filled full of raine:

7 From strength to strength they go: to God
in Sion all appeare.

8 Lord God of hoasts, o heare my pra'yr,
o Iacobs

o Iacobs God, give eare.   Selah.

(2)

9 Behould o God our shield: the face
   of thine annoynted see.
10 For better's in thy courts a day,
   then elswhere thousands bee:
   I rather had a doore-keeper
   be it'h house of my God:
   then in the tents of wickednes
   to settle mine aboad.
11 Because the Lord God is a Sun,
   he is a shield also:
   Iehovah on his people grace
   and glory will bestow:
   No good thing will he hould from them
   that doe walk uprightlee.
12 O Lord of hoasts, the man is blest
   that puts his trust in thee.

Psalme 85

To the chiefe musician, a psalme for the
   sonnes of Korah.

O LORD, thou hast been to the land
   gracious: Iacobs captiuity
thou hast returned with thy hand.
2   Thou also the iniquity
   of thy people hast pardoned:
   thou all their sin hast covered.   Selah.
3   Thou all thine anger didst withdraw:
   from thy fierce indignation
   thou hast thy selfe turned away.
4   O God of our salvation
              W   convert

convert thou us; & doe thou make
thine anger toward us to flake.

5 Shall thy wrath ever be us on?
wilt thou thine indignation
draw out to generation?
and unto generation?

6 Wilt thou not us reviv'd let bee
that thy folk may rejoyce in thee.

(2)

7 Lord on us shew thy mercy; eke
thy saving health on us bestow.

8 I'le hark what God the Lord will speak,
for hee'l speak peace his folk unto,
and to his Saints: but let not them
to foolishnes returne agen.

9 Surely his saving health is nigh
unto all them that doe him feare;
that in our land may dwell glory.

10 Mercy & truth met *together*,
prosperity & righteousnes
embracing did *each other* kiss.

11 Truth springs out of the earth: also
from heaven looketh righteousnes.

12 Yea, God shall that that's good bestow
our land eke shall give her increase.

13 Iustice shall goe before his face,
& in the way her steps shall place.

Another of the same

O LORD, thou favour'd hast thy land:
Iacobs captivity.

2 Thou hast brought back: thou pard'ned hast

thy

thy folks iniquity:
Thou haſt cloſe coverd all their ſin.

3   Thy wrath away all caſt
thou haſt: from fiercenes of thine ire
    thy ſelfe return'd thou haſt.

4 Convert us back, o thou the God
    of our ſalvation:
& toward us cauſe thou to ceaſe
    thine indignation,

5 Wilt thou be angry ſtill with us
    for evermore? what ſhall?
thine anger be by thee drawne-out
    to generations all?

6 Wilt thou not us revive? in thee
    thy folk rejoyce ſhall ſo.

7 Shew us thy mercy, Lord; on us
    thy ſaving health beſtow.

(2)

8 I'le heare what God the Lord will ſpeak:
    for to his people peace
hee'l ſpeak, & to his Saints: leſt they
    returne to foolishnes.

9 Surely naere them that doe him feare
    is his ſalvation:
that glory may within our land
    have habitation.

10 Mercy & truth doe joyntly meet:
    juſtice & peace doe kiſſe.

11 Truth ſprings from earth: & rightouſnes
    from heaven looking is.

12 Yea what is good the Lord ſhall give:

and yeild her fruit our land.

23 Iustice shall 'fore him goe: & make
    her steps i'th way to stand.

Psalme 86

A prayer of David.

Bow downe o Lord, thine eare,
    & harken unto mee:
because that I afflicted am,
    also I am needie.

2   Doe thou preserve my soule,
    for gracious am I:
o thou my God, thy servant save,
    that doth on thee rely.

3   Lord pitty me, for I
    daily cry thee unto.

4 Rejoyce thy servants soule: for Lord,
    to thee mine lift I do.

5   For thou o Lord, art good,
    to pardon prone withall:
and to them all in mercy rich
    that doe upon thee call.

6   Iehovah, o doe thou
    give eare my pray'r unto:
& of my supplications
    attend the voyce also.

7   In day of my distresse,
    to thee I will complaine:
by reason that thou unto mee
    wilt answer give againe.

(2)

8   Amongst the gods, o Lord,

none is there like to thee:
neither with thine are any work
   that may compared bee.

9   All nations o Lord,
   whom thou haft made, *the fame*
fhall come & worfhip thee before:
   and glorify thy Name.

10   Becaufe thou mighty art,
   the things that thou haft done
are wonderfull, thou art thy felfe
   the mighty God alone.

11   Iehovah, unto mee
   o make thy way appeare,
walk in thy truth I will; mine heart
   unite thy name to feare.

12   Withall mine heart I will
   o Lord my God, thee prayfe:
& I will glorify thy name,
   for evermore *alwayes.*

13   Becaufe that unto mee
   thy mercy doth excell;
alfo thou haft delivered
   my foule from loweft hell.

(3)

14   O God, the proud, & troups
   of violent rofe 'gainft mee,
after my foule they fought: nor have
   before them placed thee.

15   But Lord thou art a God,
   tender, & gracious;
longfuffring, & in mercy thou

W 2   and

& truth art plenteous.

16   O turne thou unto mee,
    and mercy on mee have:
unto thy servant give thy strength:
    thine handmaides son do save.

17   Mee shew a signe for good,
    that mine haters may see,
and be asham'd; because Lord, thou
    dost help, & comfort mee.

Psalme 87
A psalme or song for the sonnes
of Korah.

A Mong the holy hills
    is his foundation.

2 More then all Iacobs tents, the Lord
    loves the gates of Sion.

3   Things glorious spoken are
    o Gods citty, of thee.   Selah.

4 I'le mention Rahab, & Babel,
    to them that doe know mee;
    Behold Philistia,
    Tyrus *citty* likewise,
with Ethiopia; that this man
    by birth did thence arise.

5   Also it shall be sayd,
    of Sion that borne there
this & that man was, & the high'st
    himselfe shall stablish her.

6   Iehovah he shall co unt,
    ev'n at that time when as,
the people he doth number up,

that

that there this man borne was.   Selah

7   Both those that singers are
    as also *there shall bee,*
those that on instruments doe play:
    all my springs are in thee.

Psalme 88

A song or psalme for the sons of Korah, to
the chief musician uprō Mahalath Leannoth,
    Maschil of Heman the
        Ezrahite.

LORD God of my salvation,
  before thee day & night cryde I.
2 Before thee o let my pray'r come:
    incline thine eare unto my cry.
3   Because my soule is troubled so:
    and my life draws nigh to the grave.
4 Counted with them to'th pit that go:
    I'me as a man that no strength have.
5   Free among those men that be dead,
    like slaine which in the grave are shut;
    by thee noe more remembered:
    and by thy hand off are they cut.
6   Thou hast mee layd i'th pit most low
    in dakrnesses, within deep caves.
7 Hard on mee lyes thy wrath, & thou
    dost mee afflict with all thy waves.   Selah.
8   Men that of mine acquaintance bee
    thou hast put far away mee fro:
    unto them loathsome thou madst mee,
    I am shut up nor forth can go.
9   Because of mine affliction,

                    mine

mine eye with mourning pines away:
Iehovah, I call thee upon:
& stretch my hands to thee all day;

(2)

10 Shew wonders to the dead wilt thou?
shall dead arise & thee confess? Selah.

11 I'th grave wilt thou thy kindenes show?
in lost estate thy faithfullues?

12 Thy works that wonderfull have been
within the dark shal they be knowne?
& shall thy righteousnes *be seene*
in the land of oblivion?

13 But Lord I have cryde thee unto
at morne, my pray'r prevent shall thee.

14 Lord why casts thou my soule thee fro?
why hidest thou thy face from mee?

15 I'me poore afflicted, & to dye
am ready, from my youthfull yeares,
I am sore troubled doubtfully
while I doe beare thy horrid feares.

16 Thy fierce wrath over mee doth goe,
thy terrors they doe mee dismay.

17 Encompasse mee about they doe,
close mee together all the day.

18 Lover & friend a far thou hast
removed off away from mee,
& mine acquaintance thou hast cast
into darksom obscuritee.

Psalme 89
Maschil of Ethan the
Ezrahite.

PSALM

THe mercyes of Iehovah sing
   for evermore will I:
I'le with my mouth thy truth make known
   to all posterity.

2 For I have sayd that mercy shall
   for ever be up built;
establish in the very heav'ns
   thy faithfullnes thou wilt.

3 With him that is my chosen one
   I made a covenant:
& by *an oath* have sworne unto
   David mine owne servant.

4 To perpetuity thy seed
   establish-sure I will:
also to generations all
   thy throne I'le build up *still.*   Selah.

5 Also the heav'ns thy wonders Lord,
   they shall with prayse confess;
in the assemblie of the Saints
   also thy faithfullnes.

6 For who can be compar'd unto
   the Lord the heav'ns within?
'mong sonnes of mighty to the Lord
   who is't that's like to him.

(2)

7 I'th Saints assemblie greatly God
   is to be had in feare:
and to be reverenc't of all those
   that round about him are.

8 Lord God of hoasts, what Lord like thee
   in power doth abide?

thy faithfullnes doth compaſſe thee
    alſo on every ſide.
9 Over the raging of the ſea,
    thou doſt dominion beare:
when as the waves therof ariſe,
    by thee they ſtilled are.
10 Like to one ſlaine, thou broken haſt
    in pieces Rahab quite:
thou haſt diſperſt thine enemies
    ev'n by thine arme of might.
11 The heav'ns together with the earth,
    thine are they: thine they bee;
the world, with fullnes of the ſame,
    founded they were by thee.
12 The North together with the South
    thou didſt create the ſame:
Tabor together with Hermon,
    rejoyce ſhall in thy Name.

(3)

13 Thou haſt a very mighty arme,
    thy hand it is mighty,
and alſo thy right hand it is
    exalted up on high.
14 Iuſtice & judgement of thy throne
    are the prepared place:
mercy & truth preventing ſhall
    goe forth before thy face.
15 O bleſſed are the people that
    the joyfull ſound doe know,
Lord, in thy countenances light
    they up & downe ſhall goe:

16 They

16 They shall in thy name all the day
    rejoyce exceedingly:
and in thy righteousnes they shall
    be lifted up on high.

17 Because that thou art unto them
    the glory of their powre:
our horne shall be exalted high,
    also in thy favour.

18 Because Iehovah is to us
    a safe protection;
and he that is our Soveraigne,
    is Isr'ells Holy-one.
(4)

19 Then didst thou speake in vision,
    unto thy Saint, & sayd,
I upon one that mighty is
    salvation have layd:
One from the folk chose, I set up.

20 David my servant I
have found: him I annoynted with
    mine oyle of sanctity.

21 With whom my hand shall stablisht be;
    mine arme him strengthen shall.

22 Also the enemy shall not
    exact on him at all:
Nor shall the Son of wickednes
    afflict him any more.

23 Before him I'le beat downe his foes,
    and plague his haters sore.

24 My mercy, truth, shall be with him;
    & in my name shall be

his

25 his horne exalted. And I'le set
        his hand upon the sea:
    I'th rivers also his right hand.

26   He shall cry mee unto,
        thou art my Father: & my God,
            Rock of my health also.

27 Also I will make him to be
        my first begotten one:
    higher then those that Princes are,
        who dwell the earth upon.

28 My mercy I will keep for him
        to times which ever last:
    also my covenant with him
        it shall stand very fast.

(5)

29 And I will make his seed indure
        to perpetuitee:
    his throne likewise it like unto
        the dayes of heav'n shall bee.

30 If that his sons forsake my law,
        & from my judgements swerve:

31 If they my stattutes break, & my
        commandes doe not observe:

32 Then will I visit with the rod
        their bold transgression,
    as also their iniquity
        with sore stripes *them upon*.

33 But yet my loving kindenes, it
        I'le not take utterly
    away from him: nor will suffer
        my faithfullnes to lye.

34 The covenant I made with him
    by mee shall not be broke:
neither will I alter the thing
    which by my lips is spoke.

35 Once sware I by my holines,
    if I to David lye:

36 His seed asuredly shall last
    to perpetuity:
And like the Sun 'fore mee his throne.

37   It like the moone for aye
shall be establish't, like a true
    witnesse in heav'n: Selah.

(6)

38 But thou hast cast off, & us had
    in detestation:
exceedingly thou hast been wroth
    with thine annoynted one.

39 Thou hast made voyd the covenant
    of thy servant, his crowne
thou hast prophan'd unto the ground
    by casting of it downe.

40 Thou hast broke all his hedges downe:
    his forts thou ruin'd hast.

41 All those doe make a spoyle of him
    who by the way have past:
Hee's a reproach to his neighbours.

42   Of them that him annoy
thou hast advanced their right hand:
    & made all's foes to joy.

43 The sharp edge also of his sword
    thou hast turn'd backward quite:

    and

and in the battell thou haſt not
    made him to ſtand upright.
44 Thou haſt made alſo for to ceaſe
    his glorious renowne:
unto the very earth his throne
    thou alſo haſt caſt downe.
45 And of his youthfull yeares the dayes
    thou haſt diminiſhed;
with very great confuſion
    thou haſt him covered.   Selah.

(7)

46 How long? Iehovah, wilt thou hide
    thy ſelfe for evermore?
burne like unto conſuming fire
    ſhall thy diſpleaſure ſore?
47 To thy remembrance doe thou call
    how ſhort a time have I;
wherefore haſt thou created all
    mens ſonnes to vanity?
48 What ſtrong man is there that doth live,
    & death ſhall never ſee?
from the ſtrong power of the grave
    ſhall he his ſoule ſet free?
49 Thy former loving kindeneſſes
    o Lord, where are they now?
which in thy truth & faithfullnes
    to David thou didſt vow.
50 Lord, the reproach of thy ſervants
    unto remembrance call:
how I it beare in my boſome
    from mighty people all.

51 Wher-

51 Wherewith thy adverſaryes Lord,
    have caſt reproach upon,
  wherewith they have reproacht the ſteps
    of thine annointed one.
52 O let Iehovah be bleſſed
    to all eternitee:
  Amen, *ſo let it be*, alſo
    Amen, *ſo it ſhall bee.*

THE

FOVRTH BOOKE

Pſalme 90.

A prayer of Moſes the man of God.

O LORD, thou haſt been unto us
    from generation,
to generation, a place
    of fixed manſion.
2 Before the mountaines were brought forth,
    ere earth & world by thee
  were form'd: thou art eternally
    God to eternitee.
3 Thou doſt unto deſtruction
    turne miſerable men:
  and then thou ſayſt yee ſonnes of men
    doe yee returne agen.
4 For why o Lord, a thouſand yeares
    are but within thy ſight
  as yeſterday when it is paſt:

and

and as a watch by night.

5 By thee like as it were a flood
    they quite away are borne,
  they like a sleep, & as the grasse
    that grows up in the morne.

6 It in the morning flourisheth,
    it also up doth grow;
  it in the ev'ning is cut downe
    it withereth also.

7 Because wee by thine anger are
    consumed speedily:
  and by thy sore displeasure wee
    are troubled suddenly.

8 Thou hast set our iniquityes
    before thee in thy sight:
  our secret evills are within
    thy countenances light.

9 Because in thine exceeding wrath
    our dayes all passe away:
  our years wee have consumed quite,
    ev'n as a tale *are they*.

(2)

10 Threescore & ten yeares are the dayes
    of our yeares which remaine,
  & if through strength they fourscore be,
    their strength is grief & paine:
  For it's cut off soone, & wee flye
11 away: Who is't doth know
  thine angers strength? according as
    thy feare, thy wrath is so.

12 Teach us to count our dayes: our hearts

so wee'l on wisdome set.

13 Turne Lord, how long? of thy servants
let it repent thee yet?

14 O give us satisfaction
betimes with thy mercee:
that so rejoyce, & be right glad,
through all our dayes may wee.

15 According to the dayes *wherin*
affliction wee have had,
and yeares *wherin* wee have seen ill,
now also make us glad.

16 Vnto those that thy servants be
doe thou thy work declare:
also thy comely glory to
those that thy children are.

17 Let our Gods beauty be on us,
our handy works also
stablish on us; our handy work
establish it doe thou.

Psalme 91.

HE that within the secret place
of the most high doth dwell,
he under the Almightyes shade
shall lodge himselfe *full well.*

2 My hope he is, & my fortresse,
I to the Lord will say:
he is my God; & I in him
my confidence will stay.

3 Surely out of the fowlers snare
he shall deliver thee,
also thee from the Pestilence

V

infect-

infectious ſhall free.

4 He with his feathers hide thee ſhall,
    under his wings ſhall bee
thy truſt: his truth ſhall be a ſhield
    and buckler unto thee.

5 Thou ſhalt not be diſmaide with feare
    for terrour by the night:
nor for the arrow that with ſpeed
    flyeth in the day light:

6 Nor for the Peſtilence that doth
    walk in the darknes faſt:
nor for the ſore deſtruction
    that doth at noone day waſt.

(2)

7 A thouſand ſhall fall at thy ſide,
    & ten thouſand alſo
at thy right hand, but it ſhall not
    approach thee neere unto:

8 Only thou with thine eyes this thing
    attentively ſhalt view :
alſo thou ſhalt behold how that
    the wicked have their due.

9 Becauſe Iehovah who hath been
    my ſafe protection,
ev'n the moſt high, thou haſt him made
    thine habitation.

10 Not any thing that evill is
    there ſhall to thee befall,
neither ſhall any plague come nigh
    thy dwelling place at all.

11 Becauſe that he his Angells will

                   comand

command concerning thee:
in all thy wayes *where thou dost* walk
   thy keeper for to bee.
12 They shall support thee in their hands:
   lest thou against a stone
13 shouldst dash thy foot. Thou trample shalt
   on th'Adder, & Lion:
The Lion young & Dragon thou
   shalt tread under thy feet.
14 I will deliver him, for hee
   on mee his love hath set:
Because that he hath knowne my **Name**,
   I will him set on high.
15 Vpon mee he shall call in pray'r,
   and answer him will I:
I will be with him when he is
   in troublesome distresse,
& I to him will honour give,
   when I shall him release.
16 With dayes of long continuance
   I'le give to him his fill:
& also my salvation
   declare to him I will.

Psalme 92.
A psalme or song for the
Sabbath day.

IT is a good thing to give thanks
  Iehovah thee unto:
unto thy Name prayses to sing,
   o thou most high also.
2 Thy loving kindenes to shew forth

Y 2

with-

within the morning light:
also thy truth, & faithfullnes,
 to shew forth every night.

3 Vpon a ten string'd instrument,
 and Psaltery upon:
upon the solemne sounding Harp,
 a meditation.

4 For through thy work, o Lord, thou hast
 mee caused to rejoyce:
and in the workings of thy hands
 I will triumph with voyce.

5 O Lord, how mighty are thy works:
 thy thoughts are very deepe.

6 The bruitish knows not, nor the foole
 this in his heart doth keepe.

7 When as the wicked doe sprirg up
 ev'n like the grasse unto,
& all that work iniquity
 when as they flourish do:
It's that they then may be destroy'd
 to perpetuity.

8 But thou Iehovah dost abide
 for evermore most high.

9 For loe, thy foes, for loe, o Lord,
 thy foes they perish shall:
the workers of iniquity
 they shall be scattred all.

(2)

10 But like the Vnicornes my horne
 thou shalt exalt on high:
& with fresh oyle in mine old age

annoynted

annoynted be shall I.

11 Also mine eye shall see my wish
    upon mine enemyes:
mine eare shall heare of wicked ones,
    that up against me rise.

12 Like to the Palme tree flourish shall
    he that is righteous:
like to a Ceadar he shall grow
    that is in Lebanus.

13 They that within Iehovahs house
    are planted *stedfastly*:
within the Courts of our God they
    shall flourish *pleasantly*.

14 Their fruit they shall in their old age
    continue forth to bring:
they shall be fat, yea likewise they
    shall still be flourishing:

15 To shew that upright is the Lord:
    my refuge strong is hee,
also that there is not in him
    any iniquitee.

Psalme 93.

THe Lord reigns, cloth'd with majesty:
    God cloath'd with strength, doth gird
himselfe: the world so stablisht is,
    that it cannot be stir'd.

2 Thy throne is stablished of old:

3   from aye thou art. Their voyce
the flouds lift up, Lord, flouds lift up,
    the flouds lift up their noyse.

4 The Lord on high then waters noyse

more ftrong then waves of fea:

5 Thy words moft fure: Lord, holines
becomes thine houfe for aye.

Pfalme 94

O LORD God, unto whom there doe
revenges appertaine:
o God, to whom vengeance belongs,
clearly fhine forth againe.

2 Exalt thy felfe, o thou that art
Iudge of the earth throughout:
render a recompence unto
all thofe that are fo ftout.

3 Iehovah, o how long fhall they
that doe walk wickedly?
how long fhall thofe that wicked are
rejoyce triumphingly?

4 How long fhall thofe men utter forth
& fpeake things that hard bee?
& fhall all fuch thus boaft themfelves
that work iniquitee?

5 Lord, they thy folk in pieces break:
& heritage oppreſs.

6 They flay the widdow, & ftranger,
& kill the fatherlefs.

7 The Lord they fay, yet fhall not fee:
nor Iacobs God it minde.

8 Learne vulgar Sots: alfo yee fooles
when will yee wifdome finde?

9 Who plants the eare, fhall he not heare?
who formes the eye, not fee?

10 Who heathen fmites, fhall he not check?

mans

mans teacher, knows not hee?

(2)

11 The Lord doth know the thoughts of man,
    that they are very vaine.
12 Blest man whom thou correctst, o Lord;
    & in thy law dost traine.
13 That thou mayst give him quiet from
    dayes of adversity:
untill the pit be digged for
    such as doe wickedly.
14 Because Iehovah he will not
    his people cast away,
neither will hee forsake his owne
    inheritance for aye.
15 But judgement unto righteousues
    it shall returne agen:
also all upright ones in heart
    they shall pursue it *then*.
16 Against the evill doers, who
    will up for mee arise?
who will stand up for mee 'gainst them
    that work iniquityes?
17 Had not the Lord me helpt: my soule
    had neere in silence dwel'd.
18 When as I sayd, my foot slips: Lord,
    thy mercy mee upheld.

(3)

19 Amidst the multitude of thoughts
    of mine within my minde,
still from thy consolations
    my soule delight doth finde.

20 Shall the throne of iniquity
      have fellowship with thee:
  which frameth molestation
      and that by a decree?

21 They joyntly gathered themselves,
      together they withstood
  the soule of him that righteous is:
      & condemne guiltlesse blood.

22 But yet Iehovah unto mee
      he is a refuge high:
  also my God he is the rock
      of my hopefull safety.

23 Their mischief on them he shall bring,
      & in their wickednesse
  he shall them cut off : yea, the Lord
      our God shall them suppresse.

Psalme 95.

O Come, let us unto the Lord
      shout loud with singing voyce.
  to the rock of our saving health
      let us make joyfull noyse.

2 Before his presence let us then
      approach with thanksgiving:
  also let us triumphantly
      with Psalmes unto him sing.

3 For the Lord a great God: & great
      King above all gods is.

4 In whose hands are deepes of the earth,
      & strength of hills are his

5 The sea to him doth appertaine,
      also he made the same:

and

& also the drye land is his
for it his hands did frame.

6 O come, & let us worship give,
& bowing downe adore:
he that our maker is, the Lord
o let us kneele before.

7 Because he is our God, & wee
his pasture people are,
& of his hands the sheep: to day
if yee his voyce will heare,

8 As in the provocation,
o harden not your heart:
as in day of temptation,
within the vast desart.

9 Whē mee your fathers tryde, & pro'vd,
& my works lookt upon:

10 Fourty yeares long I griev'd was with
this generation:
And sayd, this people erre in heart:
my wayes they doe not know.

11 To whom I sware in wrath: if they
into my rest should goe.

Psalme 96.

SIng to the Lord a new song: sing
all th'earth the Lord unto:

2 Sing to Iehovah, blesse his Name,
still his salvation show.

3 To'th heathen his glory, to all
people his wonders spread.

4 For great's the Lord, much to be prays'd,
above all gods in dread.

Z   5 Because

5 Becaufe vaine Idols are they all
  which heathens Gods doe name:
 but yet Iehovah he it is
  that did the heavens frame.

6 Honour & comely majefty
  abide before his face:
 both fortitude & beauty are
  within his holy place.

7 Yee kindreds of the people *all*
  unto the Lord afford,
 glory & mightynes alfo
  give yee unto the Lord.

8 The glory due unto his name
  give yee the Lord unto;
 offer yee an oblation,
  enter his courts alfo.

(2)

9 In beauty of his holynes
  doe yee the Lord adore:
 the univerfall earth *likewife*
  in feare ftand him before.

10 'Mong heathens fay, Iehovah reigns:
  the world in ftablenes
 fhall be, unmov'd alfo: he fhall
  judge folk in righteoufnes.

11 O let the heav'ns *therat* be glad,
  & let the earth rejoyce:
 o let the fea, & it's fullnes
  with roaring make a noyfe.

12 O let the field be full of joye,
  & all things there about:

        then

then all the trees that be i'th wood
they joyfully shall shout
13 Before Iehovah, for he comes,
he comes earths judge to bee.
the world with justice, & the folke
judge with his truth shall hee.

Psalme 97

THe Lord doth reigne, the earth
o let heerat rejoyce:
the many Isles with mirth
let them lift up their voyce.

2   About him round
dark clouds there went,
right & judgement
his throne doe found.

3 Before him fire doth goe,
& burnes his foes about.

4 The world was light also
by lightnings he sent out:
the earth it saw
& it trembled.

5 The hills melted
like wax away
At presence of the Lord:
at his presence who is
of all the earth the Lord.

6 That righteousnes of his
the heavens high
they doe forth show:
all folk also
see his glory.

Z 2   7 who

7 Who graven Images
doe serve, on them remaine
let dreadfull shamefullnes:
& who in Idols vaine
themselves doe boast:
with worship bow
to him all you
Gods Angells *hoast*.

8 Sion heard, & was glad,
glad Iudahs daughters were,
this cause, o Lord, they had,
thy judgements did appeare.

9 For Lord thou high
all earth set o're:
all Gods before
in dignity.

10 Yee that doe love the Lord,
the evill hate doe yee;
to his Saints soules afford
protection doth hee:
he will for them
freedome command
out of the hand
of wicked men.

11 For men that righteous are
surely there is sowne light:
& gladnes for their share
that are in heart upright.

12 Ioy in the Lord,
yee Iust confesse;
his holynesse

while

while yee record.
Psalme 98.
A Psalme

A New song sing unto the Lord,
  for wonders he hath done:
his right hand & his holy arme
  him victory hath wonne.

2 Iehovah his salvation
  hath made for to be knowne:
his righteousnes i'th heathens sight
  hee openly hath showne.

3 To Isr'ells house of his mercy
  & truth hath mindefull been:
the ends of all the earth they have
  our Gods salvation seene.

4 Vnto Iehovah all the earth,
  make yee a joyfull noyse:
make yee also a cheerfull sound,
  sing prayse, likewise rejoyce.

5 With Harp sing to the Lord; with Harp,
  also with a Psalms voyce.

6 With Trumpets, Cornets sound; before
  the Lord the King rejoyce.

7 The sea let with her fullnes roare:
  the world, & there who dwell.

8 O let the flouds clap hands: let hills
  rejoyce together well

9 Before the Lord, for he doth come
  to judge the earth: rightly
with justice shall he judge the world,
  & folk with equity.

Z 3   PSALM

Psalme 99.

IEHOVAH 'tis that reigns,
   let people be in dread:
    'midst Cherubs he remaines,
   th'earth let itbe moved.

2   Iehovah is
   in Sion great,
   in highnes set
    he is likewise
   Above all the people.

3   Let them confesse thy Name
   so great & terrible:
   for holy is the same.

4   The King his might
   doth love justice:
   thou dost stablish
    things that be right:
   Iudgement thou dost, also
   in Iacob righteousnes.

5   The Lord our God doe you
   set up in his highnes,
    & worship yee
   his footstoole at:
   by reason that
    holy is hee.

6   Moses also Aron
   among his Priests, likewise
   Samuell all those among
   that to his name send cryes:
    called they have
   the Lord upon,

and

and he *alone*
  them anſwer gave.

7 He unto them did ſpeake
  it'h cloudy pillar: *then*
  they kept his records, eke
  his ord'nance he gave them.

8 Lord, thou who art
  our God didſt heare,
  & didſt anſwer
    to them impart,
  Thou waſt a God pard'ning
  them, although thou vengeance
  upon their works didſt bring.

9 The Lord our God advance,
    & bow yee downe
  at's holy hill:
  for our God's *ſtill*
    the Holy-one.

Pſalme 100.
A *Pſalme* of prayſe.

Make yee a joyfull ſounding noyſe
  unto Iehovah, all the earth:
2 Serve yee Iehovah with gladnes:
  before his preſence come with mirth.
3 Know, that Iehovah he is God,
  who hath us formed it is hee,
  & not our ſelves: his owne people
  & ſheepe of his paſture are wee.
4 Enter into his gates with prayſe,
  into his Courts with thankfullnes:
  make yee confeſſion unto him,

and

& his name reverently bleſſe.

5   Becauſe Iehovah he is good,
for evermore is his mercy:
& unto generations all
continue doth his verity.

Another of the ſame.

MAke yee a joyfull noyſe unto
  Iehovah all the earth:

2 Serve yee Iehovah with gladnes:
    before him come with mirth.

3 Know, that Iehovah he is God,
    not wee our ſelves, but hee
hath made us: his people, & ſheep
    of his paſture are wee.

4 O enter yee into his gates
    with prayſe, & thankfullneſſe
into his Courts: confeſſe to him,
    & his Name doe yee bleſſe.

5 Becauſe Iehovah he is good,
    his bounteous-mercy
is everlaſting: & his truth
    is to eternity.

Pſalme 101.

A pſalme of David.

MErcy & judgement I will ſing,
  Lord, I will ſing to thee.

2 I'le wiſely doe in perfect way:
    when wilt thou come to mee?
I will in midſt of my houſe walk
    in my hearts perfectnes:

3 I will not ſet before mine eyes

matter of wickednes:
I hate their worke that turne aside,
    it shall not cleave mee to.

4 Froward in heart from mee shall part,
    none evill will I know.

5 I'le cut him off, that slaundereth
    his neighbour privily:
I cannot beare the proud in hearr,
    nor him that looketh high.

6 Vpon the faithfull in the land
    mine eyes shall be, that they
may dwell with mee: he shall mee serve
    that walks in perfect way.

7 Hee that a worker is of guile,
    shall not in my house dwell:
before mine eyes he shall not be
    setled, that lies doth tell.

8 Yea, all the wicked of the land
    early destroy will I:
to cutt off from Gods citty all
    that work iniquity.

Psalme 102

A prayer of the afflicted when he is over-
whelmed, & poureth out his complaint
    before the Lord.

LORD, heare my supplication,
    & let my cry come thee unto:

2 I'th day when trouble is on mee,
    thy face hide not away mee fro:
Thine eare to mee doe thou incline,
    i'th day I cry, soone answer mee:

A a

3 For

3 For as the smoake my dayes consume,
   & like an hearth my bones burnt bee.

4   My heart is smote, & dryde like grasse,
   that I to eate my bread forget:

5 By reason of my groanings voyce
   my bones unto my skin are set.

6   Like Pelican in wildernes,
   like Owle in desart so am I:

7 I watch, & like a sparrow am
   on house top solitarily.

8   Mine enemies daily mee reproach:
   'gainst mee they rage, 'gainst mee they sweare:

9 That I doe ashes eate for bread:
   & mixe my drink with weeping-teare.

10   By reason of thy fervent wrath
   & of thy vehement-disdaine:
   for thou hast high advanced mee,
   & thou hast cast mee downe againe.

(2)

11   My dayes as shaddow that decline:
   & like the withered grasse am I.

12 But thou, Lord, dost abide for aye:
   & thy Name to eternity.

13   Thou wilt arise, & wilt shew forth
   thy tender-mercy on Sion:
   for it is time to favour her,
   yea the set time is now come on.

14   For in her stones thy servants doe
   take pleasure, & her dust pitty.

15 And heathens shall the Lords Name feare:
   & all Kings of th'earth thy glory.

                 16 when

16   When as the Lord shall Sion build
hee in his glory shall appeare.

17   The poor's petition hee'l regard,
& hee will not despise their pray'r.

18   This shall in writing be inroll'd
for the succeeding-after-race:
that people also which shall bee
created, they the Lord may prayse.

19   For from his Sanctuary high
from heavn's the Lord the earth doth see:

20   To heare the groanes of prisoners:
to loose them that deaths children bee.

21   The Lords prayse in Ierusalem:
his Name in Sion to record.

22   when people are together met,
& Kingdomes for to serve the Lord.

(3)

23   He weakned hath i'th way my strength,
& shortened my dayes hath hee.

24   I sayd, in middest of my dayes
my God doe not away take mee:
Thy yeares throughout all ages are.

25   Thou hast the earth's foundation layd
for elder time: & heavens bee
the work which thine owre hands have made.

26   They perish shall, but thou shalt stand:
they all as garments shall decay:
& as a wearing-vestiment
thou shalt the change, & chang'd are they.

27   But thou art ev'n the same: thy yeares
they never shall consumed bee.

23 Thy servants children shall abide,
  & their seed stablisht before thee.

Psalme 103.

A psalme of David.

O Thou my soule, Iehovah blesse,
  & all things that in me
most inward are, in humblenes
  his Holy-Name blesse ye

2 The Lord blesse in humility,
  o thou my soule: also
put not out of thy memory
  all's bounties, thee unto.

3 For hee it is who pardoneth
  all thine iniquityes:
he it is also who healeth
  all thine infirmityes.

4 Who thy life from destruction
  redeems: who crowneth thee
with his tender compassion
  & kinde benignitee.

5 Who with good things abundantlee
  doth satisfie thy mouth:
so that like as the Eagles bee
  renewed is thy youth.

6 The Lord doth judgement & justice
  for all oppressed ones.

7 To Moses shew'd those wayes of his:
  his acts to Isr'ells sonnes.

(2)

8 The Lord is mercifull also
  hee's very gracious:

and

and unto anger hee is flow,
    in mercy plenteous.

9 Contention he will not maintaine
    to perpetuity:
nor he his anger will retaine
    unto eternity.

10 According to our fins *likewife*
    to us hee hath not done:
nor hath he our iniquityes
    rewarded us upon.

11 Becaufe even as the heavens are
    in height the earth above:
fo toward them that doe him feare
    confirmed is his love.

12 Like as the Eaft & *We*ft they are
    farre in their diftances:
he hath remov'd away fo far
    from us our trefpaffes.

13 A fathers pitty like unto,
    which he his fonnes doth beare:
like pitty doth Iehovah fhow
    to them that doe him feare.

14 For he doth know this frame of ours:
    he minds that duft wee bee.

15 Mans dayes are like the graffe: like flowrs
    in field, fo flourifheth hee.

16 For over it the winde doth paffe,
    & it away doth goe;
alfo the place wheras it was
    noe longer fhall it know.

        17 But

(3)

17 But yet Gods mercy ever is,
    shall be,& aye hath been
  to them that feare him; and's justice
    unto childrens children.

18 To such as keepe his covenant,
    that doe in minde up lay
  the charge of his commandement
    that it they may obey.

19 The Lord hath in the heavens hye
    established his throne:
  and over all his Royallty
    doth beare dominion.

20 O yee his Angells that excell
    in strength, blesse yee the Lord,
  that doe his word, that harken well
    unto the voyce of 's word.

21 All yee that are the Lords armies,
    o blesse Iehovah *still*:
  & all yee ministers of his,
    his pleasure that fullfill.

22 Yea, all his works in places all
    of his dominion,
  blesse yee Iehovah: o my Soul,
    Iehovah blesse *alone*.

Psalme 104.

THe Lord blesse,o my Soule, o Lord
    my God, exceedingly
  great art thou: thou with honour art
    cloath'd & with majesty.

2 Who dost thy selfe with light, as if

it

it were a garment cover:
who like unto a curtaine doſt
the heavens ſtretch all over.

3 Who of his chambers layes the beames
ith waters, & hee makes
the cloudes his Charrets, & his way
on wings of winde hee takes.

4 His Angells Spirits, his miniſters
who makes a fiery flame.

5 who earths foundations layd, that ne're
ſhould be remov'd the ſame.

6 Thou with the deep (as with a robe)
didſt cover the *dry land*:
above the places mountainous
the waters they did ſtand.

7 When as that thou rebukedſt them
away then fled they faſt:
they alſo at thy thunders voyce
with ſpeed away doe haſt.

8 Vp by the mountaines they aſcend:
downe by the valleys go,
the place which thou didſt found for them
untill they come unto.

9 Thou haſt to them a bound prefixt
which they may not paſſe over:
ſo that they might noe more returne
againe the earth to cover.

(2)

10 who ſprings into the valleys ſends,
which run among the hills.

11 whence all beaſts of the field have drink:

wilde

wilde asses drink their fills.

12 Heavns fowles dwell by them, which do sing
 among the sprigs with mirth.

13 Hee waters from his lofts the hills:
 thy works fruit fill the earth.

14 For beasts hee makes the grasse to grow,
 herbs also for mans good:
that hee may bring out of the earth
 what may be for their food:

15 Wine also that mans heart may glad,
 & oyle their face to bright:
and bread which to the heart of man
 may it supply with might.

16 Gods trees are sappy: his planted
 Cedars of Lebanon:

17 Where birds doe nest: as for the Storke,
 Fitres are her mansion.

18 The wilde Goates refuge are the hills:
 rocks Conies doe inclose.

19 The Moone hee hath for seasons set,
 the Sun his setting knows.

(3)

20 Thou makest darknes, & 'tis night:
 when wood beasts creep out all.

21 After their prey young Lions roare:
 from God for food they call.

22 The Sun doth rise, then in their dennes
 they couch, when gone aside.

23 Man to his work & labour goes,
 untill the ev'ning-tide.

24 O Lord, how many are thy works!

all of them thou haſt wrought
in wiſdome: with thy plenteous ſtore
the earth is fully fraught.

25 So is this great & ſpatious ſea,
wherin things creeping bee
beyond all number: beaſts of ſmall
& of great quantitee.

26 There goe the ſhips: Leviathan,
therin thou madſt to play.

27 Theſe all wayt on thee, that their meate
in their time give thou may.

23 They gather what thou giveſt them:
thy hand thou op'neſt wide,
& they with ſuch things as are good
are fully ſatiſſyde.

29 Thou hia'ſt thy face, they troubled are,
their breath thou tak'ſt away,
then doe they dye: alſo returne
unto their duſt doe they.

30 They are created, when thou makſt
thy ſpirit forth to go:
thou of the earth doſt make the face
to be renew'd alſo.

(4)

31 The glory of Iehovah ſhall
for evermore indure:
in his owne works Iehovah ſhall
joyfully take pleaſure.

32 The earth doth tremble, when that hee
upon the ſame doth look,
the mountaines he doth touch, likewiſe

Bb   they

they therupon do smoak.

34 Full sweet my meditation
concerning him shall be:
so that I in Iehovah will
rejoyce *exceedinglee*.

35 Let sinners be consum'd from th'earth,
& wicked be no more:
blesse thou Iehovah, o my soule,
prayse yee the Lord *therefore*.

Psalme 105.

O Prayse the Lord, call on his Name.
mong people shew his facts.

2 Sing unto him, sing psalmes to him:
talk of all's wondrous acts.

3 Let their hearts joy, that seek the Lord:
boast in his Holy-Name.

4 The Lord seek, & his strengh: his face
alwayes seek yee *the same*.

5 Those admirable works that hee
hath done remember you:
his wonders, & the judgements which
doe from his mouth *issue*.

6 O yee his servant Abrahams seed:
sonnes of chose Iacob yee.

7 He is the Lord our God: in all
the earth his judgements bee.

8 His Covenant for evermore,
and his comanded word,
a thousand generations to
he doth in minde record,

9 Which he with Abraham made, and's oath

10　to Isack. Made it faſt,
　a law to Iacob: & Iſr'ell
　　a Cov'nant aye to laſt.
(2)
11　He ſayd, I'le give thee Canans land:
　　by lot, heirs to be there.
12　When few, yea very few in count
　　and ſtrangers in't they were;
13　When they did from one nation
　　unto another paſs:
　when from one Kingdome their goings
　　to other people was,
14　*He* ſuffred none to doe them wrong:
　　Kings checkt he for their ſake:
15　Touch not mine oynted ones; none ill
　　unto my Prophets make.
16　He cal'd for Famine on the land,
　　all ſtaffe of bread brake hee.
17　Before them ſent a man: Ioſeph
　　ſold for a ſlave to bee.
18　*W*hoſe feet they did with fetters hurt:
　　in yr'n his ſoule did lye.
19　Vntill the time that his word came:
　　the Lords word did him trye.
20　The King the peoples Ruler ſent,
　　looſ'd him & let him go.
21　He made him Lord of all his houſe:
　　of all's wealth ruler too:
22　At's will to binde his *P*eers: & teach
23　　his Ancients ſkill. Then came
　Iſr'ell to Egypt: & Iacob

B b 2　　　　　ſojourn'd

sojourn'd i'th land of Ham.

24 Hee much increaſt his folk: & made
    them ſtronger then their foe,

25 Their heart he turn'd his folk to hate
    to's ſervants craft to ſhow.

(3)

25 Moſes his ſervant he did ſend:
    & Aaron whom he choſe.

27 His ſignes & wonders them amongſt,
    they in Hams land diſcloſe.

28 Hee darknes ſent, & made it dark:
    nor did they's word gain-ſay.

29 Hee turn'd their waters into bloud:
    & he their fiſh did ſlay.

30 Great ſtore of Frogs their land brought forth
    in chambers of their Kings.

31 He ſpake, there came mixt ſwarmes, & lice
    in all their coaſts *he brings*.

32 He gave them haile for raine: & in
    their land fires flame did make.

33 And ſmote their Vines & their Figtrees:
    & their coaſt-trees he brake.

34 He ſpake, & then the Locuſts came:
    & Caterpillars, ſuch
the number of them was as none
    could reckon up how much,

35 And ate all their lands herbs: & did
    fruit of their ground devoure.

36 All firſt borne in their land he ſmote:
    the chief of all their powre.

(4)

37 With silver also & with gold
   he them from thence did bring:
  & among all their tribes there was
   not any one weak ling.

38 Egypt was glad when out they went:
   for on them fell their dread.

39 A cloud for cov'ring, & a fire
   to light the night he spred.

40 They askt, & he brought quailes: did them
   with heav'ns bread satisfy,

41 He op't the rock and waters flow'd:
   flouds ran in places dry.

42 For on his holy promise, hee
   and's servant Abraham thought.

43 With joye his people, and with songs
   forth he his chosen brought.

44 He of the heathen people did
   the land on them bestow:
  the labour of the people they
   inherited also:

45 To this intent that his statutes
   they might observe *alwayes*:
  also that they his lawes might keepe.
   doe yee Iehovah prayse.

Psalme 106.

PRayse yee the Lord, o to the Lord
   give thanks, for good is hee:
  for his mercy continued is
   to perpetuitee.

2 Who can the Lords strong acts forth tell?

Bb 3   or

or all his prayse display?

3 Blest they that judgement keep: & who
doth righteousnes alway.

4 With favour of thy people, Lord,
doe thou remember mee:
and mee with that salvation
visit which is of thee:

5 To see thy chosens good, to joy
in gladnes of thy nation:
that with thine owne inheritance
I might have exultation.

6 As our fore-fathers so have wee
sinned erroniously:
wee practis'd have iniquity,
wee have done wickedly.

(2)

7 Our fathers did not understand
thy wonders in Egypt,
nor was thy mercyes multitude
in their remembrance kept:
But at the sea at the red sea

8 vext him. Yet for his owne
Names sake he sav'd them: that he might
his mighty powre make knowne.

9 The red sea also he rebuk't,
and dryed up it was:
so that as through the wildernes,
through depths he made them pass.

10 And from the hand of him that did
them hate, he set them free:
and them redeemed from his hand

that

that was their enemee.

11 The waters covered their foes:
of them there was left none.

12 They did believe his word; they sang
his prayses therupon.

(3)

13 They soone forgot his words; nor would
they for his counsell stay:

14 But much i'th wildernes did lust;
i'th desart God tryde they.

15 And he their suite them gave; but sent
leannes their soule into.

16 They envi'd Moses in the camp,
Aaron Gods Saint also.

17 The opned earth, Dathan devour'd;
and hid Abirams troup.

18 And fire was kindled in their rout:
flame burnt the wicked up.

19 In Horeb made a calfe; also
molt image worshipt they.

20 They chang'd their glory to be like,
an oxe that eateth hay.

21 They God forgot their saviour; which
in Egipt did great acts:

22 Works wondrous in the land of Ham:
by th'red sea dreadfull facts.

23 And sayd he would them waste; had not
Moses stood (whom he chose)
'fore him i'th breach, to turne his wrath,
lest that hee should waste *those*.

(4)

24 Yet they despis'd the pleasant land:
 nor did believe his word:

25 But murmur'd in their tents: the voyce
 they heard not of the Lord.

26 To make them fall i'th desart then,
 'gainst them he lift his hands.

27 'Mongst nations eke to fell their seed,
 and scatter them i'th lands.

28 And to Baal-Peor they joyn'd themselves:
 ate offrings of the dead.

29 Their works his wrath did thus provoake:
 the plague amongst them spread.

30 Then Phineas rose, & judgement did:
 and so the plague did stay.

31 Which justice to him counted was:
 to age and age for aye.

(5)

32 At th'waters of contention
 they angred him also:
 so that with Moses for their sakes,
 it _very_ ill did go:

33 Because his spirit they provoakt:
 with's lips to speake rashly.

34 The nations as the Lord them charg'd,
 they stroyd not utterly:

35 But were amongst the Heathen mixt,
 and learn'd their works to do:

36 And did their Idols serve; which them
 became a snare unto.

37 Yea, unto divills, they their sonnes

and

and daughters offered.

38 And guiltlesse bloud, bloud of their sons
& of their daughters shed,
Whom unto Canans Idols they
offred in sacrifice :
the land with bloud abundantly
polluted was likewise.

39 Thus with the works were they defylde
which they themselves had done:
and they did goe a whoring with
inventions of their owne:

(6)

40 Therefore against his folk the wrath
was kindled of the Lord:
so that he the inheritance
which was his owne abhorr'd.

41 And he gave them to heathens hand;
their haters their lords were.

42 Their foes thral'd them; under their hand
made them the yoake to beare.

43 Oft he deliverd them; but they
provoakt him bitterly
with their counsell, & were brought low
for their iniquity.

44 Yet, he regarded their distresse;
when he did heare their plaint.

45 And he did to remembrance call
for them his Covenant:
And in his many mercyes did

46 repent. And made them bee
pitty'd of all that led them forth

Cc

into

into captivitee.

47 Save us, o Lord our God, & us
from heathens gath'ring rayse
to give thanks to thy Holy-Name:
to triumph in thy prayse.

48 The Lord the God of Israell
from aye to aye blest bee:
and let all people say Amen.
o prayse Iehovah yee.

THE

Fift Booke

Psalme 107.

O Give yee thanks unto the Lord,
because that good is hee:
because his loving kindenes lasts
to perpetuitee.

2 So let the Lords redeem'd say: whom
hee freed from th'enemies hands:

3 And gathred them from East, & *West*,
from South, & Northerne lands.

4 I'th desart, in a desart way
they wandred: no towne finde,

5 to dwell in. Hungry & thirsty:
their soule within them pinde.

6 Then did they to Iehovah cry
when they were in distresse:
who did them set at liberty

out of their anguishes.

7 In such a way that was most right
he led them forth also:
that to a citty which they might
inhabit they might go.

8 O that men would Iehovah prayse
for his great goodnes *then*:
& for his workings wonderfull
unto the sonnes of men.

9 Because that he the longing soule
doth throughly satisfy:
the hungry soule he also fills
with good abundantly.

(2)

10 Such as in darknes' and within
the shade of death abide;
who are in sore affliction,
also in yron tyde:

11 By reason that against the words
of God they did rebell;
also of him that is most high
contemned the counsell.

12 Therefore with molestation
hee did bring downe their heart:
downe did they fall, & none their was
could help to them impart.

13 Then did they to Iehovah cry
when they were in distress:
who did them set at liberty
out of their anguishes.

14 He did them out of darknes bring,

also

also deaths shade from under:
as for the bands that they were in
    he did them break asunder.

15 O that men would Iehovah prayse
    for his great goodnes *then*:
and for his workings wonderfull
    unto the sonnes of men.

15 For he hath all to shivers broke
    the gates that were of brasse:
& hee asunder cut each barre
    that made of yron was.

(3)

17 For their transgressions & their sins,
    fooles doe affliction beare.

18 All kinde of meate their soule abhorres:
    to deaths gate they draw neare.

19 Then did they to Iehovah cry
    when they were in distress:
who did them set at liberty
    out of their anguishes.

20 He, sent his word, & therewithall
    healing to them he gave:
from out of their destructions
    he did them also save.

21 O that men would Iehovah prayse,
    for his great goodnes *then*:
& for his workings wonderfull
    unto the sons of men.

22 And sacrifices sacrifice
    let them of thanksgiving:
& while his works they doe declare

let them for gladnes sing.

(4)

23 They that goe downe to'th sea in ships:
 their busines there to doo

24 in waters great. The Lords work see,
 it'h deep his wonders too.

25 Because that he the stormy winde
 commandeth to arise:
which lifteth up the waves therof,

26 They mount up to the skyes:
Downe goe they to the depths againe,
 their soule with ill doth quaile.

27 They reele,& stagger,drunkard like,
 and all their witt doth faile.

28 Then did they to Iehovah cry
 when they were in distress:
and therupon he bringeth them
 out of their anguishes.

29 Hee makes the storme a calme: so that
 the waves therof are still.

30 Their rest then glads them; he them bring
 to'th hav'n which they did will.

31 O that men would Iehovah prayse
 for his great goodnes *then*:
& for his workings wonderfull
 unto the sons of men.

32 Also within the peoples Church
 him let them highly rayse:
where Elders are assembled,there
 him also let them prayse.

(5)

33 He rivers to a defart turnes,
    to drought the fpringing well:
34 A fruitfull foyle to barrennes;
    for their fin there that dwell.
35 The defart to a poole he turnes;
    and dry ground to a fpring.
36 Seates there the hungry; who prepare
    their towne of habiting,
37 Vineyards there alfo for to plant,
    alfo to fow the field;
which may unto them fruitfull things
    of much revenue yield.
33 Alfo he bleffeth them, fo that
    they greatly are increaft:
and for to be diminifhed
    he fuffers not their beaft.
39 Againe they are diminifhed
    & they are brought downe low,
by reafon of their preffing-ftreights,
    affliction & forrow.

(6)

40 On Princes he contempt doth powre;
    and caufeth them to ftray
i'th folitary wildernes,
    wherin there is no way.
41 Yet hee out of affliction
    doth make the poore to rife:
& like as if it were a flock
    doth make him families.
42 The righteous fhall it behold,

                                    and

and he shall joyfull bee:
in silence stop her mouth also
shall all iniquitee.

43 Who so is wise, & who so will
these things attentive learne:
the loving-kindenes of the Lord
they clearely shall discerne.

Psalme 108.

A song or psalme of David.

O GOD, my heart's fixt, I'le sing; prayse
sing ev'n with my glory.

2 Awake thou Psaltery & Harp;
I will awake early.

3 O thou Iehovah, thee will I
the people prayse among:
within the midst of nations
thee will I prayse with song.

4 For o're the heav'ns thy mercys great;
to'th skyes thy truth doth mount.

5 Or'e heav'ns o God, be lift, all earth
let thy glory surmount:

6 That thy beloved people may
be set at libertee:
with thy right hand salvation give,
& doe thou answer mee.

(2)

7 God hath in his *owne* holines
spoken, rejoyce I shall:
of Shechem I'le division make;
& mete out Succoths vale.

8 Mine Gilead, mine Manasseh is,

and

& Ephraim also hee
is of my head the strength: Iudah
   shall my law-giver bee.

9 Moab my wash-pot, I will cast
   over Edom my shoo:
I'le make a shout triumphantly
   over Philistia too.

10 Who is it that will bring me to
   the citty fortifyde?
who is it that into Edom
   will be to mee a guide?

11 Wilt not thou doe this thing, o God,
   who didst us cast thee fro?
& likewise wilt not thou o God,
   forth with our armies go?

12 From trouble give us help; for vaine
   is mans salvation.

13 Through God wee shall do valiantly;
   for hee'l our foes tread downe.

Psalme 109.

To the chief musician, a psalme
of David.

GOD of my prayse, hold not thy peace,
  For mouth of the wicked,
& mouth of the deceitfull are
   against mee opened:
Gainst mee they speake with lying tongue.

3   And compasse mee about
with words of hate; & mee against
   without a cause they fought.

4 They for my love mine enemies are:

but

but I my prayer make.

5 And ill for good rewarded mee
   & hate for my loves sake.

6 A wicked person over him
   doe thou make for to sit,
also at his right hand doe thou
   let Satan stand at it.

7 When he is judged, let him then
   condemned be therin:
and let the prayr that hee doth make.
   be turned into sin.

8 Few let his dayes bee: & let his
   office another take.

9 His children let be fatherlesse,
   and's wife a widow make.

10 Let's children still be vagabonds,
   begge they their bread also:
out of their places desolate
   let them a seeking go.

(2)

11 Yea, let th'extortioner catch all
   that doth to him pertaine:
and let the stranger spoyle what he
   did by his labour gaine.

12 Let there not any bee that may
   mercy to him expresse:
nor any one that favour may
   his children fatherlesse.

13 The issue also let thou be
   cut off that from him came:
it'h following generation

Dd

out

out blotted be his name.

14 Remembred with the Lord be his
　　fathers iniquitee:
and of his mother never let
　　the sin out blotted bee.

15 Before Iehovah let them bee
　　continually put:
that from out of the earth he may
　　the mem'ry of them cut.

16 Because that he remembred not
　　compassion to impart,
but did pursue the needy poore:
　　to slay the broke in heart.

(3)

17 As he did cursing love, so let
　　cursing unto him come:
as he did not in blessing joy,
　　so be it far him from.

18 With cursing like a robe as hee
　　cloath'd him: so let it go
like water to his bowels, and
　　like oyle his bones into.

19 Garment like let it to him be,
　　himselfe for to aray:
and for a girdle, wherewith hee
　　may gird himselfe alway.

20 Thus let mine adversaryes bee
　　rewarded from the Lord:
also of them against my soule
　　that speak an evil word.

21 But

(4)

21 But God the Lord, for thy Names sake,
   o doe thou well for mee:
because thy mercy it is good,
   o doe thou set mee free.

22 For poore & needy I: in mee
   my heart's wounded also.

23 Like falling shade I passe: I'me tost
   Locust like to & fro.

24 Through fasts my knees are weak: my flesh
   it's fatnes doth forsake.

25 And I am their reproach: they look
   at mee, their heads they shake.

26 Help mee, o Lord my God: after
   thy mercy save thou mee:

27 That they may know this is thy hand:
   Lord that i'ts done by thee.

28 Let them curse, but o doe thou blesse;
   when as that they arise
let them be shamed, thy servant
   let him rejoyce likewise.

29 Mine adversaryes o let them
   with shame be cloath'd upon:
& themselves cloath as with a cloak
   with their confusion.

30 I'le to Iehovah with my mouth
   give thanks exceedingly:
yea him among the multitude
   with prayse I'le glorify.

31 For hee shall stand at right hand of
   the poore & needy one:

from

from thoſe that doe condemne his ſoule
to give ſalvation.

Pſalme 110.

A pſalme of David.

THe Lord did ſay unto my Lord,
  ſit thou at my right hand:
till I thine enemies make a ſtoole
  wheron thy feet may ſtand.

2 The Lord the rod ſhall of thy ſtrength
    ſend from out of Sion:
  in middeſt of thine enemies
    have thou dominion.

3 Willing thy folk in thy dayes powre,
    in holy beautyes bee:
  from mornings womb; thou haſt the dew
    of thy youth unto thee.

4 Iehovah ſware, nor will repent,
    thou art a Prieſt for aye:
  after the order that I of
    Melchizedeck did ſay.

5 The Lord who is at thy right hand.
    wounding ſhall ſtrike through Kings
  in that ſame day wherin that hee
    his indignation brings.

6 Hee ſhall among the heathen judge,
    and fill with bodies dead
  great places, & o're many lands
    he ſhall ſtrike through the head.

7 Out of the torrent he ſhall drink
    i'th way *hee paſſeth by*:
  becauſe of this therefore hee ſhall

liſt

lift up his head on hye.

Psalme iii.

PRayse yee the Lord: with my whole heart
　Iehovah prayse will I:
　　i'th private meetings of th'upright,
　　and publicke assembly.

2 Great are the Lords works: sought of all
　　that in them have pleasure.

3 Comely & glorious is his work:
　　aye doth his justice dure.

4 To be remembred he hath made
　　his doings merveilous:
　full of compassion is the Lord
　　as well as gracious.

5 Meate hath hee given unto them
　　that fearers of him bee:
　he evermore his covenant
　　doth keepe in memoree:

6 The power of his works hee did
　　unto his people show:
　that he the heathens heritage
　　upon them might bestow.

(2)

7 Both verity & judgement are
　　the working of his hands:
　yea very faithfull also are
　　each one of his commands.

8 For ever & for evermore
　　they stand in stablenes:
　yea they are done in verity
　　also in uprightnes.

Dd 3

9 Redemption

9 Redemption to his folk he sent,
   that covenant of his
for aye he hath ordaind: holy
   and reverend his Name is.

10 Of wisdome the begining is
   Iehovahs feare : all they
that doe his will have prudence good:
   his prayse indures for aye.

Pſalme 112.

PRayse yee the Lord. bleſt is the man
   that doth Iehovah feare,
that doth in his commandements
   his ſpirit greatly cheare.

2 The *very* mighty upon earth
   ſhall be that are his ſeed:
they alſo ſhall be bleſſed that
   from th'upright doe proceed.

3 And there ſhall be within his houſe
   both wealth & much rich ſtore:
his righteouſnes it alſo doth
   indure for evermore.

4 In midſt of darknes there doth light
   to upright ones ariſe:
both gracious, & pittyfull,
   righteous he is likewiſe.

(2)

5 A good man hee doth favour ſhow
   & ready is to lend:
and with deſcretion his affayres
   he carryes to an end.

6 That man ſhall not aſſuredly

for ever moved bee:
the righteous man he shall be had
in lasting memoree.

7 By evill tydings that he heares
he shall not be afrayd:
his trust he putting in the Lord.
his heart is firmly stayd.

8 His heart is sure established,
feare shall not him surprise,
untill he see what hee desires
upon his enemies.

9 He hath disperst, hath giv'n to poore:
his justice constantly
indureth: & his horne shall be
with honour lifted hye.

10 The wicked shall see, & be griev'd;
gnash with his teeth shall hee
and melt away: and their desire
shall faile that wicked bee.

Psalme 113.

THe Lord prayse yee, prayse yee the Lord
his servants Gods Name prayse.

2 O blessed be Iehovahs Name,
from henceforth & alwayes.

3 From rising to the setting sun:
the Lords Name's to be praysd.

4 The Lord all nations is above:
o're heav'ns his glory raysd

5 Who is like to, the Lord our God?
who upon earth doth dwell.

6 Who humble doth himselfe to view.

in

in heav'n, in earth as well.

7 The needy from the dust he lifts:
   the poore lifts from the dung.

8 That hee with princes may him set:
   his peoples Peeres among.

9 The barren woman he doth make
   to keepe house, & to bee
a joyfull mother of children:
   wherefore the Lord prayse yee.

Psalme 114.

VVHen Isr'ell did depart
   th'Egyptians from among,
and Iacobs house from a people
   that were of a strange tongue:

2   Iudah his holy place:
   Isrell's dominion was.

3 The sea it saw, & fled: Iordane
   was forced back to pass.

4   The mountaines they did leap
   upwards like unto rams:
the litle hills also they did
   leap up like unto lambs.

5   Thou sea what made thee flye?
   thou Iordane, back to go?

6 Yee mountaines that yee skipt like rams:
   like lambs yee hills also?

7   Earth at Gods presence dread,
   at Iacobs Gods presence:

8 The rock who turnes to waters lake:
   springs he from flint sends thence.

Pſalme 115

NOt to us, not unto us, Lord,
 but glory to thy Name afford:
 for thy mercy, for thy truths ſake.
2 The heathen wherefore ſhould they ſay:
where is their God now gone away?
3 But heavn's our God his ſeat doth make:
Hee hath done whatſoe're he would.
4 Their Idols are ſilver & gold:
 the handy work of men they were.
5 Mouths have they, ſpeachleſſe yet they bee:
eyes have they, but they doe not ſee.
6 Eares have they but they doe not heare:
Noſes have they, but doe not ſmell.
7 Hands have they, but cannot handell,
 feet have they but they doe not go:
And through their throat they never ſpake.
8 Like them are they, that doe them make:
 & all that truſt in them are ſo.
9 Truſt in the Lord o Iſraell,
he is their help, their ſhield as well.
10 O Arons houſe the Lord truſt yee:
Hee is their help, & hee their ſhield.
11 Who feare the Lord, truſt to him yield:
 their help alſo their ſhield is hee.

(2)

12 The Lord hath mindefull been of us,
he'le bleſſe us, he'le bleſſe Iſr'ells houſe:
 bleſſing he'le Arons houſe afford.
13 He'le bleſſe Gods fearers: great & ſmall.
14 You & your ſons, the Lord much ſhall

Ee
 increaſe

15 increase still. You blest of the Lord
16 which heav'n & earth made. Heav'ns heav'ns
the Lords: but th'earth mens sons gives hee. (bee
17 The Lords prayse dead doe not afford:
Nor any that to silence bow.
18 But wee will blesse the Lord both now
and ever henceforth. prayse the Lord.

Psalme 116.

I Love the Lord, because he doth
my voice & prayer heare.
2 And in my dayes will call, because
he bow'd to mee his eare.
3 The pangs of death on ev'ry side
about beset mee round:
the paines of hell 'gate hold on mee,
distresse & griefe I found.
4 Vpon Iehovahs Name therefore
I called, *& did say,*
deliver thou my soule, o Lord,
I doe thee humbly pray.
5 Gracious the Lord & just, our God
is mercifull also.
6 The Lord the simple keeps: & hee
sav'd mee when I was low.
7 O thou my soule doe thou returne
unto thy quiet rest:
because the Lord to thee himselfe
hath bounteously exprest.
8 For thou hast freed my soule from death,
mine eyes from teares, from fall
9 my feet. Before the Lord i'th land

of

of living walk I shall.

(2)

10 I did believe, therefore I spake:
     afflicted much was I.

11 That every man a lyar is
     I did say hastily.

12 What shall I render to the Lord,
     to mee for's benefits all.

13 I'le take the cup of saving health
     & on the Lords Name call.

14 In presence now of all his folk,
     I'le pay the Lord my vowes.

15 Of his Saints, in Iehovahs sight
     the death is pretious.

16 I am thy servant, truly Lord
     thine owne servant am I:
   I am the son of thy hand-maide,
     my bands thou didst untye.

17 Of thanksgiving the sacrifice
     offer to thee I will:
   Iehovahs Name I earnestly
     will call upon it still.

18 Vnto Iehovah I will pay
     the vowes were made by mee,
   now in the presence of all them
     that his owne people bee.

19 Within the Courts of the Lords house,
     ev'n in the midst of thee
   o thou *citty* Ierusalem:
     o prayse Iehovah yee.

Psalme 117.

E e 2   PSALM

ALl nations, prayſe the Lord; him prayſe
all people. For his mercies bee
great toward us: alſo alwayes
the Lords truth laſts. the Lord prayſe yee.
Another of the ſame.

AL nations, prayſe the Lord; all folk
prayſe him. For his mercee
is great to us; & the Lords truth
aye laſts. the Lord prayſe yee.
Pſalme 118.

O Give yee thanks unto the Lord,
becauſe that good is hee;
becauſe his loving kindenes laſts
to perpetuitee.

2 For ever that his mercie laſts
let Iſraell now ſay.

3 Let Arons houſe now ſay, that his
mercie indures for aye.

4 Likewiſe let them now ſay, who of
Iehovah fearers bee;
his loving kindenes that it laſts
to perpetuitee.

5 I did lift up my voice to God
from out of ſtreitnes great;
the Lord mee anſwerd, & mee plac't
in an inlarged ſeat.

6 The Lord's for mee, I will not feare
what man can doe to mee.

7 Iehovah takes my part with them
that of mee helpers bee:
Therefore upon them that mee hate

my

my wishes see shall I.
8 'Tis better to trust in the Lord:
   then on man to rely.
(2)
9 'Tis better to trust on the Lord:
   then trust in Princes put.
10 All nations compast mee; but them
   in Gods Name I'le off cut.
11 They compast mee about, yea they
   mee compassed about:
but in Iehovahs Name I will
   them utterly root out.
12 They compast mee like Bees, are quencht
   like as of thornes the flame:
but I will utterly destroy
   them in Iehovahs Name.
13 Thou didst thrust sore to make mee fall:
   the Lord yet helped mee.
14 The Lord my fortitude & song:
   & saving health is hee.
15 The tabernacles of the just
   the voice of joye afford
& of salvation: strongly works
   the right hand of the Lord.
16 The right hand of Iehovah is
   exalted up on hye:
the right hand of Iehovah is
   a working valiantly.
(3)
17 I shall not dye, but live: & tell
   what things the Lord worketh.

E e 3   18 The

18 The Lord did sorely chasten mee:
       but gave mee not to death.

19 O set wide open unto mee
       the gates of righteousnes:
    I will goe into them, & will
       Iehovahs praise confess.

20 This same Iehovahs gate at which
       the just shall enter in.

21 I'le praise thee, for thou hast mee heard,
       and hast my safety bin.

22 The stone which builders did refuse
       head corner stone now lyes.

23 This is the doing of the Lord:
       it's wondrous in our eyes,

                    (4)

24 This is the very day the which
       Iehovah hee hath made:
    wee will exceedingly rejoyce,
       & in it will be glad.

25 Iehovah I doe thee beseech,
       salvation now afford:
    I humbly thee intreat, now send
       prosperity, o Lord.

26 Hee that comes in Iehovahs Name
       o let him blessed bee:
    out of Iehovahs house to you
       a blessing with doe wee.

27 God he Iehovah is, and hee
       light unto us affords:
    the sacrifices binde unto
       the altars hornes with cords.

                                    Thou

28 Thou art my God, & I'le thee prayſe,
my God I'le ſet thee hye.

29 O prayſe the Lord, for he is good,
and aye laſts his mercy.

Pſalme 119.

א   (1)   Aleph

ALL-bleſt are men upright of way:
walk in Iehovahs law who do.

2 Bleſt ſuch as doe his records keepe:
with their whole heart him ſeek alſo.

3 And that work no iniquitie:
but in his wayes doe walke *indeed.*

4 Thou haſt giv'n charge, with diligence
unto thy precepts to give heed.

5 Ah that to keepe thy ſtatutes: ſo
my wayes addreſſed were by thee.

6 When I reſpect thy precepts all,
then ſhall I not aſhamed bee.

7 Whē I thy righteous judgements learne
with hearts uprigutnes I'le thee prayſe.

8 Forſake thou mee not utterly:
I will obſerve thy ſtatute-wayes.

ב   (2)   Beth

9 By what may 'young man cleanſe his way?
by heeding it as thy word guides.

10 With my whole heart thee have I ſought:
thy lawes let mee not goe beſides.

11 I in my heart thy word have hid:
that I might not againſt thee ſin.

12 Thou o Iehovah, bleſſed art:
thine owne ſtatutes inſtruct mee in.

13 All

13 All the juſt judgements of thy mouth
    declared with my lips have I.

14 I in thy teſtimonyes way
    joy more then in all rich plenty.

15 In thy precepts I'le meditate:
    and have reſpect unto thy wayes.

16 My ſelfe I'le ſolace in thy lawes:
    and not forget what thy word ſayes.

ﻥ (3) Gimel

17 Confer this grace thy ſervant to,
    that I may live thy word to keep.

18 Vnveile mine eyes, that I may ſee
    out of thy law the wonders deep.

19 I am a ſtranger in the earth:
    do not thy precepts from me hide.

20 My ſoule is broken with deſire
    unto thy judgements time & tide.

21 Thou haſt rebuk'd the proud, acurſt
    which doe frō thy commandments ſwerve.

22 Roll off from mee reproach & ſcorne:
    for I thy records doe obſerve.

23 Ev'n Princes ſate & 'gainſt mee ſpake;
    but on thy lawes thy ſervant muſ'd.

24 Thy records alſo are my joyes:
    and for men of my counſell uſ'd.

ﻥ (4) Daleth

25 Downe to the duſt my ſoule cleav's faſt:
    o quicken mee after thy word.

26 I ſhow'd my wayes & thou mee heardſt:
    thy ſtatutes learning mee afford.

27 Thy precepts way make mee to know:

so I'le muse on thy wondrous wayes.

28 My soule doth melt for heavines:
   according to thy word mee rayse.

29   The way of lying from mee take:
   and thy law grant mee graciously.

30 The way of truth I chosen have:
   thy judgements *fore mee* layd have I.

31   Thy testimonies cleave I to;
   o Lord, on mee shame do not cast.

32 Then shall I run thy precepts way,
   when thou mine heart enlarged hast.

E   (5)   He.

33 Enforme mee Lord, in thy laws path;
   and I will keep it to the end.

34 Skill give mee, & thy law I'le keep:
   yea with my whole heart it attend.

35   Cause mee to tread thy precepts path;
   because therin delight I do.

36 Vnto thy records bend my heart;
   & covetousnes not unto.

37   From vaine sights turne away mine eyes:
   and in thy way make mee to live.

38 Confirme thy word thy servant to,
   who to thy feare himselfe doth give.

39   My slander which I feare remove;
   because thy judgements good they bee.

40 Loe for thy precepts I have lon'gd:
   o in thy justice quicken mee.

F   (6)   Vau.

41 Finde mee out let thy mercies Lord:
   thy saving health as thou hast sayd.

42 So I my taunters answer shall,
for on thy word my hope is stayd.

43 Nor truths-word quite frō my mouth take:
because thy judgements I attend.

44 So I thy law shall alway keep,
to everlasting without end.

45 And I will walk at libertie,
because I doe thy precepts seek.

46 Nor will I blush, when before Kings
I of thy testimonies speak.

47 In thy commands, which I have lov'd,
also my selfe delight I will.

48 And lift my hands to thy commands
belov'd: & minde thy statutes still.

G (7) Sajin.

49 Good to thy servant make the word,
on which to hope thou didst mee give.

50 This was my comfort in my griefe,
because thy word doth make mee live.

51 The proud have much derided mee:
yet have I not thy law declinde.

52 Thy judgements Lord, that are of old,
I did recall, & comfort finde.

53 Horrour hath taken hold on mee:
for lewd men that thy law forsake.

54 I, in my pilgrimages house,
of thy statutes my songs doe make.

55 By night remembred I thy Name,
o Lord: & I thy law observe.

55 This hath been unto mee, because
I from thy precepts did not swerve.

Hee

ℸ (8) Heth.

57 Hee, ev'n the Lord, my portion is,
I said that I would keep thy word.

58 With my whole heart thy face I begg'd:
thy promis'd mercies mee afford.

59 I thought upon my waies, & turn'd
my feet into thy testaments.

60 I hasted, & made no delaies
to keepe with heed thy commandments.

61 The bands of wicked men mee robb'd:
of thy law I am not mindeless.

62 Ile rise at midnight thee to praise;
for judgements of thy righteousnes.

63 Companion am I to all them,
that feare thee, & thy laws doe heed.

64 Thy mercie fills the earth, o Lord:
teach mee the lawes thou hast decreed.

ഠ (9) Teth.

65 Iehovah, with thy servant thou
after thy word, right-well hast done.

66 Good taste & knowledge, teach thou mee,
for I believe thy precepts on.

67 Before I was chastis'd, I stray'd:
but I thy word observ'd have now.

68 Thou art good, & art doing good:
thy statutes teach mee, oh doe thou.

69 The proud against mee forg'd a lye:
thy laws I'le keepe with my hearts-might.

70 The heart of them is fat as grease:
but in thy law I doe delight.

71 It's good for mee, I was chastis'd:

Ff 2

that

that so thy statutes learne I should.

72 Better to mee is thy mouths-law,
then thousands of silver & gold.

K̓ (10) Iod.

73 Know make mee, & I'le learn thy lawes:
thy hands mee formed have, & made.

74 Who feare thee, mee shall see, & joy:
because hope in thy word I had.

75 Thy judgements Lord, I know are just;
& faithfully thou chastnedst mee.

76 As thou hast to thy servant spoke,
now let thy grace my comfort bee.

77 Send mee thy grace, that I may live;
for thy law as my joy I chuse.

78 Shame proud ones, that mee falsly wrong:
but I will in thy precepts muse.

79 Let them that feare thee turne to mee;
and such as have thy records knowne.

80 Let my heart bee in thy lawes sound
that so I shame may suffer none.

L ɔ (11) Caph.

81 Look for thy word I doe, *when as*
my soule doth faint for help from thee.

82 Mine eies have failed for thy word,
saying, when wilt thou comfort mee?

83 I like a smoake-dride-bottle am;
yet doe I not thy laws forgoe.

84 what are thy servants daies? when wilt
on my pursuers judgement doe?

85 The proud have digged pits for mee,
which doe not unto thy law sute.

All

86 All thy comands are truth: help mee,
  they wrongfully mee persecute.

87 They nigh had wasted mee on earth,
  but I thy laws did not forsake.

88 To keep the records of thy mouth,
  mee in thy mercie lively make.

M 7 (12) Lamed.

89 Made fast i'th heavens is thy word,
  o Lord, for ever to endure.

90 From age to age thy faithfullnes:
  thou form'dst the earth, & it stands-sure.

91 As thou ordain'dst, they still abide;
  for all are servants thee unto.

92 Had not thy law been my delight:
  Then had I perisht in my wo.

93 Thy statutes I will ne're forget:
  because by them thou quicknedst mee.

94 Thine owne am I, save mee, because
  I sought thy precepts studiouslee.

95 The wicked watch mee, mee to stroy:
  but I thy testimonies minde.

96 Of all perfection, end I see:
  but very large thy law I finde.

N D (13) Mem.

97 Now how much doe I love thy law?
  it is my study all the day.

98 Thou mad'st mee wiser then my foes
  by thy rule: for it's with mee aye.

99 I'me wiser then my teachers all:
  for thy records my study are.

100 I more then ancients understand;

F f 3   because

because I kept thy laws with care.

101   From each ill path my feet I stay'd:
    that so I might thy word observe.

102 Because thou hast instructed mee,
    I did not from thy judgements swerve.

103   How sweet are thy words to my taste?
    to my mouth more then honie they.

104 I from thy precepts wisdome learne:
    therefore I hate each lying way.

      O   (14)   Nun.

105   Of my feet is thy word the lamp:
    and to my path the shining light.

106 Sworne have I, & will it performe,
    that I will keep thy judgements right.

107   I am afflicted very much:
    Lord quicken mee after thy word.

108 Accept my mouths free-offrings now:
    & mee thy judgements teach o Lord.

109   My soule is alwaies in my hand:
    but I have not thy law forgot.

110 The wicked laide for mee a snare:
    yet from thy laws I strayed not.

111   Thy recods are mine heritage
    for aye: for my hearts joy they bee.

112 I bent my heart still to performe
    thy statues to eternitee.

      P   (15)   Samech.

113   Pursue-I doe with hatred, all
    vaine thoughts: but love thy law doe I.

114 My covert & my shield art thou:
    I on thy word wait hopefully.

115 Depart from mee, lewd men, that I
may keepe my Gods commandements.

116 By thy word stay mee, & I live:
nor shame mee for my confidence.

117 Susteine mee, & I shall be safe:
and in thy law still I'le delight.

118 thou tread'st downe all that from thy laws
doe stray: for false is their deceit.

119 All th'earths lewd ones like drosse thou-
therefore thy records love I do.   (stroyd'st

120 For feare of thee my flesh doth quake:
I doe thy judgements dread also.

Q ע (16) Hajin.

121 Quite to oppressors leave mee not:
I judgement doe, & righteousnes.

122 thy servants suretie be for good:
let not the proud ones mee oppress.

123 Mine eyes for thy salvation faile:
as also for thy righteous word.

124 In mercie with thy servant deale:
& thy lawes-learning mee afford.

125 I am thy servant, make mee wise,
thy testimonies for to know.

126 Time for thee Lord it is to work,
for men thy law doe overthrow.

127 Therefore doe I thy precepts love,
above gold, yea the finest gold.

128 All false paths hate I: for thy rules
of all things, are all right, I hold.

R ד (17) Pe.

129 Right-wondrous are thy testimonies:
                                        there-

therefore my soule keeps them with care.

130 The entrance of thy words gives light:
and makes them wise that simple are.

131   I gape & pant for thy precepts;
because I longed *for the same*.

132 Look on mee, & such grace mee show,
as thou dost them that love thy Name

133   My steps by thy word guide: & let
no wickednes beare rule in mee.

134 From mens oppression mee redeem:
and thy laws-keeper will I bee.

135   Make thy face on thy servant shine:
and mee to learne thy statutes cause.

136 Mine eies run floods of waters downe:
because they doe not keep thy laws.

S ẙ   (18)   Tzade.

137 Sincerely-just art thou, o Lord,
thy judgements upright are also.

138 Thy testimonies thou commandst
are right, yea, very faithfull too.

139   My zeale consumed mee, because
mine enemies thy words forget.

140 Thy word it is exceeding pure:
therefore thy servant loveth it.

141   Small am I, & contemptible:
yet thy commands forget not I.

142 Thy justice, justice is for aye:
also thy law is verity.

143   Distresse & anguish seas'd on mee:
yet thy commands delights mee give.

144 *Thy* records justice lasts for aye:

also

make thou mee wise, & I shall live.

T ק (19) Koph.

145   o mee that cry with my whole heart
    Lord heare: thy statutes keep I will.

146 I unto thee did cry: save mee,
    & I shall keep thy records still.

147   The dawning I prevent, & cry:
    I for thy word doe hopefull-waite.

148 Mine eyes prevent the night-watches,
    in thy word for to meditate.

149   Lord, of thy mercy heare my voice:
    after thy judgements quicken mee.

150 Who follow mischiefe, they draw nigh:
    who from thy law afarre off bee.

151   But o Iehovah, thou art neere:
    and all thy precepts verity.

152 I long since of thy records knew:
    thou laid'st them for eternity.

V ר (20) Resch.

153   iew mine affliction, & mee free:
    for I thy law doe not forget.

154 Plead thou my cause, & mee redeem:
    for thy words sake alive mee set.

155   Salvation from lewd men is far:
    sith they thy laws to finde ne're strive.

156 Great are thy bowell- mercies Lord:
    after thy judgements mee revive.

157   Many my foes and hunters are:
    yet I not from thy records swerve.

158 I saw transgressors, & was griev'd,
    for they thy word doe not observe.

Gg   See

159   See Lord, that I thy precepts love:
graunt, of thy bounty live I may.

160 Thy word's beginning it is truth:
and all thy right judgements for aye.

VV שׁ (21)   Schin.

161 ithout cause Princes mee pursue:
but of thy word my hearts in awe.

162 As one that hath much booty found,
so I rejoyce doe in thy law.

163   Lying I hate, & it abhorre:
but thy law dearly love doe I.

164 Seven times a day I prayse thee, for
the judgements of thine equity.

165   Great peace have they that love thy law:
& such shall finde no stumbling-stone.

166 I hop't for thy salvation, Lord:
and thy commandments I have done.

167   My soule thy testimonies keeps:
and them I love exceedinglee.

168 I keep thy rules & thy records:
for all my waies before thee bee.

Y ת (22)   Thau.

169 ield Lord, my cry, t'approach thy face:
as thou hast spoke, mee prudent make.

170 Let my request before thee come:
deliver mee for thy words sake.

171   My lips shall utter forth *thy* prayse:
when thou thy lawes hast learned mee.

172 My tongue shall forth thy word resound:
for all thy precepts justice *bee*.

173 To help mee let thy hand be neere:

for thy commandments chose have I.

274 I long for thy salvation, Lord:
 and my delights in thy law ly.

275 Let my soule live, & shew thy prayse:
 help mee also thy judgements let.

276 Like lost sheep strayd, thy servant seeke:
 for I thy laws doe not forget

Psalme 120.

A song of degrees.

VNto the Lord, in my distresse
 I cry'd, & he heard mee.

2 From lying lipps & guilefull tongue,
 o Lord, my soule set free.

3 What shall thy false tongue give to thee,
 or what on thee confer?

4 Sharp arrows of the mighty ones,
 with coales of juniper.

5 Woe's mee, that I in Mesech doe
 a sojourner remaine:
 that I doe dwell in tents, which doe
 to Kedar appertaine.

6 Long time my soule hath dwelt with him
 that peace doth much abhorre,

7 I am for peace, but when I speake,
 they ready are for warre.

Psalme 121.

A song of degrees.

I To the hills lift up mine eyes,
 from whence shall come mine aid.

2 Mine help doth from Iehovah come,
 which heav'n & earth hath made.

3 Hee will not let thy foot be mov'd,
   nor flumber; that thee keeps.
4 Loe hee that keepeth Ifraell,
   hee flumbreth not, nor fleeps.
5 The Lord thy keeper is, the Lord
   on thy right hand the fhade.
6 The Sun by day, nor Moone by night,
   fhall thee by ftroke *invade.*
7 The Lord will keep the from all ill:
   thy foule hee keeps alway,
8 Thy going out, & thy income,
   the Lord keeps now & aye.

Pfalme 122.

A fong of degrees.

I Ioy'd in them, that to mee fyd
   to the Lords houfe go wee.
2 Ierufalem, within thy gates,
   our feet fhall ftanding bee.
3 Ierufalem, it builded is
   like unto a citty
together which compacted is
   within it felfe clofely.
4 Whether the tribes, Gods tribes afcend
   unto Ifr'ells witnes;
that they unto Iehovahs Name
   may render thankfullnes.
5 For there the judgements thrones, the thrones
   of Davids houfe doe fit.
6 O for Ierufalem her peace
   fee that yee pray for it:
Profper they fhall that doe theelove.

7 peace

7   Peace in thy fortresses
    o let there be, prosperity
    within thy Pallaces.
8 For my brethren & for my friends,
    I'le now speake peace to thee.
9 I'le for our God Iehovahs house,
    seek thy felicitee.

Psalme 123.
A song of degrees.

O Thou that sittest in the heav'ns,
  I lift mine eyes to thee.
2 Loe, as the servants eyes unto
    hand of their masters *bee*:
  As maides eyes to her mistresse hand,
    so are our eyes unto
  the Lord our God, untill that hee
    shall mercy to us show.
3 O Lord be mercifull to us,
    mercifull to us bee:
  because that filled with contempt
    exceedingly are wee.
4 With scorne of those that be at ease,
    our soule's fill'd very much:
  also of those that great ones are,
    ev'n with contempt of such.

Psalme 124.
A song of degrees. of David.

H Ad not the Lord been on our side,
  may Israell now say,
2 Had not God been for us, when men
    did rise against us they:

                Gg 3   3 The

3 They had then swallow'd us alive,
    when their wrath on us burn'd.

4 Then had the waters us o'rewhelmd,
    the streame our soule or'e turnd.

5 The proud waters then, on our soule
    had passed on their way:

6 Blest be the Lord, that to their teeth
    did not give us a prey.

7 Our soule, as bird, escaped is
    out of the fowlers snare:
the snare asunder broken is,
    and wee delivered are.

8 The succour which wee doe injoye,
    is in Iehovahs Name:
who is the maker of the earth,
    and of the heavens frame.

psalme 125.

A song of degrees.

They that doe in Iehovah trust
    shall as mount Sion bee:
which cannot be remo'vd, but shall
    remaine perpetuallee.

2 Like as the mountaines round about
    Ierusalem doe stay:
so doth the Lord surround his folk,
    from henceforth ev'n for aye.

3 For lewd mens rod on just mens lot
    it shall not resting bee:
lest just men should put forth their hand
    unto iniquitee.

4 To those Iehovah, that be good,

gladnes

gladnes to them impart:
as also unto them that are
    upright within their heart.
5 But who turne to their crooked wayes,
    the Lord shall make them go
with workers of iniquity:
    but peace be Isr'ell to.

psalme 126.
A song of degrees.

WHen as the Lord return'd againe
    Sions captivitee:
at that time unto them that dreame
    compared might wee bee.
2 Then was our mouth with laughter fill'd,
    with singing then our tongue:
the Lord hath done great things for them
    said they, t'heathens among.
3 The Lord hath done great things for us,
    wherof wee joyfull bee.
4 As streames in South, doe thou o Lord,
    turne our captivitee.
5 Who sow in teares, shall reape in joy.
6   Who doe goe forth, & mourne,
bearing choise seed, shall sure with joye
    bringing their sheaves returne.

psalme 127.
A song of degrees for Solomon.

IF God build not the house, vainly
    who build it doe take paine:
except the Lord the citty keepe,
    the watchman wakes in vaine.

2 I'ts

2 I'ts vaine for you early to rise,
    watch late, to feed upon
  the bread of grief: so hee gives sleep
    to his beloved one.
3 Loe, the wombes fruit, it's Gods reward
    sonnes are his heritage.
4 As arrows in a strong mans hand,
    are sons of youthfull age.
5 O blessed is the man which hath
    his quiver fill'd with those:
  they shall not be asham'd, i'th gate
    when they speake with their foes.

Psalme 128.
A song of degrees.

BLessed is every one
    that doth Iehovah feare:
  that walks his wayes along.
2   For thou shalt eate *with cheare*
      thy hands labour:
    blest shalt thou bee,
    it well with thee
      shall be therefore.
3   Thy wife like fruitfull vine
    shall be by thine house side:
    the children that be thine
    like olive plants abide
      about thy board.
4   Behold thus blest
    that man doth rest,
      that feares the Lord.
5   Iehovah shall thee blesse

from

from Sion, & shalt see
Ierusalems goodnes
all thy lifes dayes that bee.

6   And shalt view well
thy children then
with their children,
    peace on Isr'ell.

Psalme 129.
A song of degrees.

FRom my youth, now may Isr'ell say,
  oft have they mee assaild:
2 They mee assaild oft from my youth,
  yet 'gainst mee nought prevaild.
3 The ploughers plough'd upon my back,
  their furrows long they drew:
4 The righteous Lord the wickeds cords
  he did asunder-hew.
5 Let all that Sion hate be sham'd,
  and turned back together.
6 As grasse on house tops, let them be,
  which ere it's grown, doth wither:
7 Wherof that which might fill his hand
  the mower doth not finde:
nor therewith hee his bosome fills
  that doth the sheaves up binde.
8 Neither doe they that passe by, say,
  Iehovahs blessing bee
on you: you in Iehovahs Name
  a blessing wish doe wee.

Psalme 130.
A song of degrees.

H h

LORD, from the depth I cryde to thee.
My voice Lord, doe thou heare:
unto my supplications voice
let be attent thine eare.

3 Lord, who should stand? if thou o Lord,
shouldst mark iniquitee.

4 But with thee there forgivenes is:
that feared thou maist bee.

5 I for the Lord wayt, my soule wayts:
& I hope in his word.

6 Then morning watchers watch for morn,
more my soule for the Lord.

7 In God hope Isr'ell, for mercy
is with the Lord: with him

8 there's much redemption. From all's sin
hee Isr'ell will redeem.

Psalme 131.

A song of degrees, of David.

MY heart's not haughty, Lord,
nor lofty are mine eyes:
in things too great, or high for mee,
is not mine exercise.

2 Surely my selfe I have
compos'd, and made to rest,
like as a child that weaned is,
from off his mothers *brest*:
Im'e like a weaned child.

3 Let Israell then stay
with expectation on the Lord,
from henceforth and for aye.

Psalme 132.

A song

PSALME CXXXII.

A song of degrees.

Remember David, Lord,
and all's affliction:
2 How to the Lord he swore, & vow'd
to Iacobs mighty one.
3   Surely I will not goe
my houses tent into:
upon the pallate of my bed,
thither I will not go.
4   I will not verily
give sleep unto mine eyes:
nor will I give to mine eye-lidds
slmber *in any wise*,
5   Vntill that for the Lord
I doe finde out a seate:
a fixed habitation,
for Iacobs God so great.
6   Behould, at Epratah,
there did wee of it heare:
ev'n in the plain-fields of the wood
wee found it *to be there*.
7   Wee'l goe into his tents:
wee'l at his footstoole bow.
8 Arise, Lord, thou into thy rest:
and th'Arke of thy strength *now*.
9   Grant that thy priests may be
cloathed with righteousnes:
0 let thy holy ones likewise
shout forth for joyfullnes.
10   Let not for Davids sake   *2 part.*
a servant unto thee,

Hh 2

the

the face of thine annoynted one
    away quite turned bee.

11 The Lord to David sware
    truth, nor will turne from it;
thy bodyes fruit, of them I'le make
    upon thy throne to sit.

12 If thy sons keep my law,
    and covenant, I teach them;
upon thy throne for evermore
    shall sit their children then.

13 Because Iehovah hath
    made choise of *mount* Sion:
he hath desired it to bee
    his habitation.

14 This is my resting place
    to perpetuity:
here will I dwell, and that because
    desired it have I.

15 Blesse her provision
    abundantly I will:
the poore that be in her with bread
    by mee shall have their fill.

16 Her Priests with saving health
    them also I will clad:
her holy ones likewise they shall
    with shouting loud be glad.

17 The horne of David I
    will make to bud forth there:
a candle I prepared have
    for mine annoynted *deare.*

18 His enemies I will

                        with

with shame apparrell them:
but flourishing upon himselfe
shall be his Diadem:

Psalme 133.

A song of degrees, of David.

How good and sweet o see,
i'ts for brethren to dwell
together in unitee:

2   It's like choise oyle *that fell*
the head upon,
that downe did flow
the beard unto,
beard of Aron:
The skirts of his garment
that unto them went downe;

3   Like Hermons dews descent,
Sions mountaines upon,
for there to bee
the Lords blessing,
life aye lasting
commandeth hee.

Annother of the same.

How good it is, o see,
and how it pleaseth well,
together ev'n in unitee
for brethren soe to dwell:

2   I'ts like the choise oyntment
from head, to'th beard did go,
downe Arons beard: downeward that went
his garments skirts unto.

3   As Hermons dew, which did

Hh 3

on Sions hill defcend:
for there the Lord bleffing doth bid,
ev'n life without an end.

Pfalme 134.

A fong of degrees.

O All yee fervants of the Lord,
  behold the Lord bleffe yee;
yee who within Iehovahs houfe
  i'th night time ftanding bee.

2 Lift up your hands, and bleffe the Lord,
  in's *place* of holines.

3 The Lord that heav'n & earth hath made,
  thee out of Sion bleff.

Pfalme 135.

THe Lord praife, praife ye the Lords Name:
  the Lords fervants o praife him yee.

2 That in the Lords houfe ftand: *the fame*
  i'th Courts of our Gods houfe who bee.

3 The Lord prayfe, for the Lord is good:
  for fweet its to his Name to fing.

4 For Iacob to him chofe hath God:
  & Ifr'ell for his pretious thing.

5 For that the Lord is great I know:
  & over all gods, our Lord keeps.

6 All that he wills, the Lord doth do:
  in heav'n, earth, feas, & in all deeps.

7 The vapours he doth them conftraine,
  forth from the ends of th'earth to rife;
he maketh lightning for the raine:
  the winde brings from his treafuries.

(2)

8   Of Egipt he the first borne smit:
and that of man, of beasts also.

9   Sent wondrous signes midst thee, Egipt:
on Pharoah, on all's servants too.

10   Who smote great natiōs, slew great Kings:

11   Slew Sihon King of th'Amorites,
Og also one of Bashans kings:
all kingdomes of the Cananites,

12   And gave their land an heritage:
his people Isr'ells lot to fall.

13   For aye thy Name, Lord, through each age
o Lord, is thy memoriall.

14   For his folks judge, the Lord is hee:
and of his servants he'le repent.

15   The heathens Idols silver bee,
& gold: mens hands did them invent.

16   Mouths have they, yet they never spake:
eyes have they, but they doe not see:

17   Eares have they, but no hearing take:
& in their mouth no breathings bee.

18   They that them make, have their likenes:
that trust in them so is each one.

19   The Lord o house of Isr'ell bless;
the Lord blesse, thou house of Aaron.

20   O house of Levi, blesse the Lord:
who feare the Lord, blesse ye the Lord.

21   From Sion blessed be the Lord;
who dwells at Salem praise the Lord.

Psalme 136,

PSALM CxxxvI.

O Thank the Lord, for hee is good:
  for's mercy lasts for aye.

2 Give thanks unto the God of gods:
  for's mercy is alway.

3 Give thanks unto the Lord of lords:
  for's mercy lasts for aye.

4 To him who only doth great signes:
  for's mercy is alway.

5 To him whose wisdome made the heav'ns:
  for's mercy &c.

6 Who o're the waters spread the earth:
  for's mercy &c.

7 Vnto him that did make great lights:
  for's mercy &c.

8 The Sun for ruliug of the day:
  for's mercy &c.

9 The Moone and Stars to rule by night:
  for's mercy &c.

10 To him who Egipts first-borne smote:
  for's mercy &c.

11 And from amongst them Isr'ell brought:
  for's mercy &c.

12 With strong hand, & with stretcht-out arme:
  for's mercy &c.

13 To him who did the red sea part:
  for's mercy &c.

14 And throngh i'ts midst made Isr'ell goe:
  for's mercy &c.

15 But there dround Pharoah & his hoast:
  for's mercy &c.

16 His people who through desart led:

                                    for's

for's mercy &c.

17 To him which did smite mighty Kings:
    for's mercy &c.

18 And put to slaughter famous Kings:
    for's mercy &c.

19 Sihon King of the Amorites:
    for's mercy &c.

20 And Og who was of Bashan King:
    for's mercy &c.

21 And gave their land an heritage:
    for's mercy &c.

22 A lot his servant Israell to:
    for's mercy &c.

23 In our low state who minded us:
    for's mercy &c.

24 And us redeemed from our foes:
    for's mercy &c.

25 Who giveth food unto all flesh:
    for's mercy lasts for ay.

26 Vnto the God of heav'n give thanks:
    for's mercy is alway.

Psalme 137.

The rivers on of Babilon
    there when wee did sit downe:
yea even then wee mourned, when
    wee remembred Sion.

2 Our Harps wee did hang it amid,
    upon the willow tree.

3 Because there they that us away
    led in captivitee,
Requir'd of us a song, & thus

I i

askt

askt mirth: us waste who laid,
sing us among a Sions song,
   unto us then they said.

4 The lords song sing can wee? being
5   in strangers land. Then let
loose her skill my right hand, if I
   Ierusalem forget.

6 Let cleave my tongue my pallate on,
   if minde thee doe not I:
if chiefe joyes or'e I prize not more
   Ierusalem my joy.

7 Remember Lord, Edoms sons word,
   unto the ground said they,
it rase, it rase, when as it was
   Jerusalem her day.

8 Blest shall hee bee, that payeth thee,
   daughter of Babilon,
who must be waste: that which thou hast
   rewarded us upon.

9 O happie hee shall surely bee
   that taketh up, that eke
thy little ones against the stones
   doth into pieces breake.

Psalme 138.
A psalme of David.

WIthall my heart, I'le prayse thee *now:*
   before the gods I'le sing to thee.
2 Toward thine holy Temple bow,
   & praise thy Name for thy mercee,
   & thy truth: for thy word thou hye
   or'e all thy Name dost magnify.

3   It'h day I cride, thou answredst mee:
    with strength thou didst my soule up-beare.

4   Lord, all the earths kings shall praise thee,
    the word when of thy mouth they heare.

5   Yea, they shall sing in the Lords wayes,
    for great's Iehovahs glorious prayse.

6   Albeit that the Lord be hye,
    respect yet hath he to the low:
    but as for them that are lofty,
    he them doth at a distance know.

7   Though in the midst I walking bee
    of trouble thou wilt quicken mee,
    Forth shalt thou make thine hand to go
    against their wrath that doe me hate;
    thy right hand shall me save also.

8   The Lord will perfect mine estate:
    thy mercy Lord, for ever stands:
    leave not the works of thine owne hands.

Another of the same.

With all my heart, I'le thee confess:
    thee praise the gods before.

2 The Temple of thine holines
    towards it I'le adore:
  Also I will confesse thy Name,
    for thy truth, & mercy:
  because thou over all thy Name
    thy word dost magnify.

3 In that same day that I did cry,
    thou didst mee answer make:
  thou strengthnedst mee with strength, which I
    within my soule *did take.*

4 O Lord, when thy mouths words they heare
   all earths Kings shall thee praise.

5 And for the Lords great glory, there
   they shall sing in his wayes.

6 Albeit that the Lord be high,
   yet hee respects the low:
but as for them that are lofty
   hee them far off doth know.

7 Though I in midst of trouble go,
   thee quickning mee I haue:
thy hand thou wilt cast on my foe,
   thy right hand shall mee saue.

8 The Lord will perfect it for mee:
   thy mercy ever stands,
Lord, doe not those forsake that bee
   the works of thine owne hands.

Psalme 139.

To the chief musician, a psalme
of David.

O LORD, thou hast me searcht & knowne.
   Thou knowst my sitting downe,
& mine up-rising: my thought is
   to thee afarre off knowne.

3 Thou knowst my paths, & lying downe,
   & all my wayes knowst well.

4 For loe, each word that's in my tongue,
   Lord, thou canst fully tell.

5 Behinde thou gird'st mee, & before:
   & layst on mee thine hand.

6 Such knowledge is too strange, too high,
   for mee to understand

7 where

7 Where shall I from thy presence go?
　　or where from thy face flye?

8 If heav'n I climbe, thou there, loe thou,
　　if downe in hell I lye.

9 If I take mornings wings; & dwell
　　where utmost sea-coasts bee.

10 Ev'n there thy hand shall mee conduct:
　　& thy right hand hold mee.

11 That veryly the darknes shall
　　mee cover, if I say:
　then shall the night about mee be
　　like to the lightsome day.

12 Yea, darknes hideth not from thee,
　　but as the day shines night:
　alike unto thee both these are,
　　the darknes & the light.

13 Because that thou possessed hast
　　my reines: *and* covered mee
　within my mothers wombe thou hast.

14 　My prayse shall be of thee,
　Because that I am fashioned
　　in fearfull wondrous wise:
　　& that thy works are merveilous,
　　my soule right well descries.

(2)

15 From thee my substance was not hid,
　　when made I was closely:
　　& when within th'earths lowest parts
　　I was wrought curiously.

16 Thine eyes upon my substance yet
　　imperfected, did look,

Ii 3

and

& all the members that I have
    were written in thy booke,
What dayes they should be fashioned:
    none of them yet were come.

17 How pretious are thy thoughts to mee,
    o God? how great's their summe?

18 If I should count them, in number
    more then the sands they bee:
& at what time I doe awake,
    still I abide with thee.

19 Assuredly thou wilt o God,
    those that be wicked slay:
yee that are bloody men, therefore
    depart from mee away.

20 Because that they against thee doe
    speake wickedly *likewise*:
thy Name they doe take up in vaine
    who are thine enemies.

21 Thy haters Lord, doe I not hate?
    & am not I with those
offended grievously that doe
    up-rising thee oppose?

22 Them I with perfect hatred hate:
    I count them as my foes.

23 Search mee o God, & know my heart:
    try mee, my thoughts disclose:

24 And see if any wicked way
    in mee there bee at all:
& mee conduct within the way
    that last for ever shall.

Palme 140

PSALME Cxl.

To the chief musician, a psalme
of David,

LORD, free mee from the evill man:
from violent man save mee.

2 Whose hearts thinke mischief: every day
for war they gathred bee.

3 Their tongues they have made to be sharp
a serpent like unto :
the poyson of the Aspe it is
under their lipps *also*.   Selah.

4 Keepe mee, Lord, from the wickeds hands,
from violent man mee save:
my goings who to overthrow
in thought projected have.

5 The proud have hid a snare for mee,
cords also: they a net
have spred abroad by the way side:
grins for mee they have set.   Selah.

6 Vnto Iehovah I did say,
thou art a God to mee:
Lord, heare the voice of my requests,
which are for grace to thee.

(2)

7 O God, the Lord, who art the stay
of my salvation:
my head by thee hath covered been
the day of battell on.

8 Those mens desires that wicked are,
Iehovah, doe not grant,
their wicked purpose furher not,
lest they themselves doe vaunt.

9 As

9 As for the head of them that mee
    doe round about inclofe,
  o let the moleftation
    of their lips cover thofe.

10 Let burning coales upon them fall,
    into the fire *likewife*
  let them be caft, into deepe pits,
    that they no more may rife.

11 Let not i'th earth eftablifht bee
    men of an evill tongue:
  evill fhall hunt to overthrow
    the man of violent wrong.

12 The afflicteds caufe, the poore mans right,
    I know God will maintaine:
13 Yea, juft fhall praife thy Name: th'upright
    fhall 'fore thy face remaine.

Pfalme 141.

A pfalme of David.

O GOD, my Lord, on thee I call,
    doe thou make haft to mee:
and harken thou unto my voice,
    when I cry unto thee.

2 And let my pray'r directed be
    as incenfe in thy fight:
and the up-lifting of my hands
    as facrifice at night.

3 Iehovah, oh that thou would'ft fet
    a watch my mouth before:
as alfo of my lips with care
    o doe thou keepe the dore.

4 Bow not my heart to evill things;

to doe the wicked deed
with wicked workers: & let not
mee of their dainties feed.

5 Let juſt-men ſmite mee, kindenes 'tis;
let him reprove mee eke,
it ſhall be ſuch a pretious oyle,
my head it ſhall not breake:
For yet my prayr's ev'n in their woes.

6 When their judges are caſt
on rocks, then ſhall they heare my words,
for they are ſweet to taſte.

7 Like unto one who on the earth
doth cutt & cleave the wood,
ev'n ſo our bones at the graves mouth
are ſcattered abroad.

8 But unto thee o God, the Lord
directed are mine eyes:
my ſoule o leave not deſtitute,
on thee my hope relyes.

9 O doe thou keepe mee from the ſnare
which they have layd for mee;
& alſo from the grins of thoſe
that work iniquitee.

10 Together into their owne nets
o let the wicked fall:
untill ſuch time that I eſcape
may make from them withall.

Pſalme 142.
Maſchil of David, a prayer when
he was in the cave.

K k

VNto Iehovah with my voice,
  I did unto him cry:
unto Iehovah with my voice
  my sute for grace made I.

2 I did poure out before his face
  my meditation:
before his face I did declare
  the trouble mee upon.

3 O'rewhelm'd in mee when was my spirit,
  then thou didst know my way:
I'th way I walkt, a snare for mee
  they privily did lay.

4 On my right hand I lookt, & saw,
  but no man would mee know,
all refuge faild mee: for my soule
  none any care did show.

5 Then to thee Lord, I cryde, & sayd,
  my hope thou art *alone*:
& in the land of living ones
  thou art my portion.

6 Because I am brought very low,
  attend unto my cry:
from my pursuers save thou mee,
  which stronger bee then I.

7 That I thy Name may praise, my soule
  from prison oh bring out:
when thou shalt mee reward, the just
  shall compasse mee about.

Psalme 143.
A psalme of David.

PSALME Cxliii.

LORD, heare my prayr, give eare when I
   doe supplicate to thee:
  in thy truth, in thy righteousnes;
    make answer unto mee.

2 And into judgement enter not
    with him that serveth thee;
  for in thy sight no man that lives
    can justified bee.

3 For th'enemie hath pursude my soule,
    my life to'th ground hath throwne:
  & made mee dwell i'th dark like them
    that dead are long agone.

4 Therefore my spirit is overwhelmd
    perplexedly in mee:
  my heart also within mee is
    made desolate to bee.

5 I call to minde the dayes of old,
    I meditation use
  on all thy words: upon the work
    of thy hands I doe muse.

6 I even I doe unto thee
    reach mine out-stretched hands:
  so after thee my soule doth thirst
    as doe the thirsty lands.   Selah.

(2)

7 Hast, Lord, heare mee, my spirit doth faile,
    hide not thy face mee fro:
  lest I become like one of them
    that downe to pit doe go.

8 Let mee thy mercy heare i'th morne,
    for I doe on thee stay,

Kk 2   wherin

wherin that I should walk cause mee
   to understand the way:
For unto thee I lift my soule.

9   O Lord deliver mee
   from all mine enemies; I doe flye
     to hide my selfe with thee.

10 Because thou art my God, thy will
     oh teach thou mee to doe,
   thy spirit is good: of uprightnes
     lead mee the land into.

11 Iehovah, mee o quicken thou
     ev'n for thine owne Names sake;
  And for thy righteousnes my soule
     from out of trouble take.

12 Doe thou also mine enemies
     cut off in thy mercy,
  destroy them that afflict my soule:
     for thy servant am I.

Psalme 144.
A psalme of David.

O Let Iehovah blessed be
    who is my rock of might,
who doth instruct my hands to war,
   and my fingers to fight.

2 My goodnes, fortresse, my hye towre,
     & that doth set mee free:
my shield, my trust, which doth subdue
     my people under mee.

3 Iehovah, what is man, that thou
     knowledge of him dost take?
what is the son of man, that thou

acount

account of him doſt make?

4 Man's like to vanity: his dayes
    paſſe like a ſhade away.

5 Lord, bow the heav'ns, come downe & touch
    the mounts & ſmoake ſhall they.

6 Lightning caſt forth, & ſcatter them:
    thine arrows ſhoor, them rout,

7 Thine hand o ſend thou from above,
    doe thou redeeme mee out:
    And rid mee from the waters great:
    from hand of ſtrangers brood:

8 Whoſe mouth ſpeaks lyes, their right hand is
    a right hand of falſehood.

(2)

9 O God, new ſongs I'le ſing to thee:
    upon the Pſaltery,
    and on ten ſtringed inſtrument
    to thee ſing praiſe will I.

10 It's hee that giveth unto Kings
    ſafety victorious:
    his ſervant David he doth ſave
    from ſword pernitious.

11 Rid mee from hand of ſtrange children,
    whoſe mouth ſpeakes vanity:
    & their right hand a right hand is
    of lying falſity:

12 That like as plants which are growne up
    in youth may be our ſons;
    our daughters pallace like may be
    polliſht as corner ſtones:

13 Our garners full, affording ſtore

of

of every fort of meates;
our cattell bringing thoufands forth,
ten thoufands in our ftreets:

14 Strong let our oxen bee to work,
that breaking in none bee
nor going out: that fo our ftreets
may from complaints bee free.

15 O bleffed fhall the people be
whofe ftate is fuch as this:
o bleffed fhall the people be,
whofe God Iehovah is.

Pfalme 145.

Davids pfalme of praife.

MY God, o King, I'le thee extoll:
& bleffe thy Name for aye.

2 For ever will I praife thy Name;
and bleffe thee every day.

3 Great is the Lord, moft worthy praife:
his greatnes fearch can none.

4 Age unto age fhall praife thy works:
& thy great acts make knowne.

5 I of thy glorious honour will
fpeake of thy majefty;
& of the operations
by thee done wondroufly.

6 Alfo men of thy mighty works
fhall fpeake which dreadfull are:
alfo concerning thy greatnes,
it I will forth declare:

7 Thy great goodneffes memory
they largely fhall exprefs:

and

and they shall with a shouting voice
  sing of thy righteousnes.

8 The Lord is gracious, & hee is
  full of compassion:
slow unto anger, & full of
  commiseration.

9 The Lord is good to all: or'e all   *part* (2)
  his works his mercies bee.

10 All thy works shall praise thee, o Lord:
  & thy Saints shall blesse thee,

11 They'le of thy kingdomes glory speake:
  and talk of thy powre *hye*;

12 To make mens sons his great acts know:
  his kingdomes majesty.

13 Thy Kingdome is a kingdome aye:
  & thy reigne lasts alwayes.

14 The Lord doth hold up all that fall:
  and all downe-bow'd ones rayse.

15 All eyes wayt on thee, & their meat
  thou dost in season bring.

16 Opnest thy hand, & the desire
  fill'st of each living thing.

17 In all his wayes the Lord is just:
  & holy in's works all.

18 Hee's neere to all that call on him:
  in truth that on him call.

19 Hee satisfy will the desire
  of those that doe him feare:
Hee will be safety unto them,
  and when they cry he'le heare.

20 The Lord preserves each one of them

                         that

that *lovers of* him bee:
but whosoever wicked are
abolish them doth hee.

21 My mouth the prayses of the **Lord**
by speaking shall expresse:
also all flesh his holy Name
for evermore shall blesse.

Psalme 146.

THe Lord praise: praise(my soule)the **Lord**.
So long as I doe live
I'le praise the Lord; while that I am,
praise to my God I'le give.

3 Trust not in Princes; nor mans son
who can no succour send.

4 His breath goe's forth,to's earth he turnes,
his thoughts that day doe end.

5 Happie is hee that hath the God
of Iacob for his ayd:
whose expectation is upon
Iehovah his God stayd.

6 Which heav'n,earth,sea,all in them made:
truth keeps for evermore:

7 Which for th'oppressed judgement doth,
gives to the hungry store,

8 The **Lord** doth loose the prisoners.
the Lord ope's eyes of blinde,
the Lord doth raise the bowed downe;
the Lord to'th just is kinde.

9 The Lord saves stangers, & relievs
the orphan, & widow:
but hee of them that wicked are

the

the way doth overthrow.
10 The Lord shall reigne for evermore,
    thy God, o Sion, hee
  to generations all shall reigne:
    o prayse Iehovah yee.

Psalme 147.

PRayse yee the Lord, for it
    is good praises to sing,
  to our God for it's sweet,
    praise is a comely thing.

2   Ierusalem
    the Lord up-reares,
    outcasts gathers
        of Isre'll *them*.

3   The broke in heart he heales:
    & up their wounds doth binde.

4   The stars by number tells:
    hee calls them all by kinde.

5   Our Lord great is,
    & of great might,
    yea infinite
        his knowledge 'tis.

6   The Lord sets up the low:
    wicked to ground doth fling.

7   Sing thanks the Lord unto
    on Harp, our Gods praise sing.

8   Who clouds the skyes,
    to earth gives raines:
    who on mountaines
        makes grasse to rise.

9   Beasts, hee & ravens young
                L l

when

when as they cry feeds then.

10 Ioyes not in horses strong:
nor in the leggs of men.

11   The Lord doth place
his pleasure where
men doe him feare,
    & hope on's grace.

12 Ierusalem, God praise:
Sion thy God confess:

13 For thy gates barres he stayes:
in thee thy sons doth bless.

14   *Peace* maketh hee
in borders thine:
with wheat so fine
    hee filleth thee.

15 On earth sends his decree:
swiftly his word doth pass.

16 Gives snow like wool, spreds hee
his hoare frost ashes as.

17   His yce doth cast
like morsels to:
'fore his cold who
    can stand stedfast?

18 His word sends, & them thaws:
makes winde blow, water flows.

19 His word, Iacob; his laws,
& judgements Isr'ell shows.

20   Hee hath so done
no nation to,
judgements also
    they have not knowne.
      Hallelujah,

PSALME Cxlviii.

Pſalme 148. Hallelujah.

FRom heav'n o praiſe the Lord:
 him praiſe the heights within.
2 All's Angells praiſe afford,
 all's Armies praiſe yee him.
3 O give him praiſe
 Sun & Moone *bright*:
 all Stars of light,
  o give him praiſe.
4 Yee heav'ns of heav'ns him praiſe:
 or'e heav'ns yee waters *cleare*.
5 The Lords Name let them praiſe:
 for hee ſpake, made they were.
6 Them ſtabliſht hee
 for ever & aye:
 nor ſhall away
  his made decree.
7 Praiſe God from th'earth *below*:
 yee dragons & each deepe.
8 Fire & haile, miſt & ſnow:
 whirl-windes his word which keepe.
9 Mountaines, alſo
 you hills all yee:
 each fruitfull tree,
  all Cedars too.
10 Beaſts alſo all cattell:
 things creeping, foules that flye.
11 Earths kings, & all people:
 princes, earths judges *hye*:
  doe all the ſame.
12 Young men & maids:

old men & babes.

13　　Praise the Lords Name,
For his Name's hye only:
　　his glory o're earth & heav'n.

14　His folks horne he lifts hye
　　the praise of all's Saints, ev'n
　　　　the sons who bee
　　of Israell,
　　his neere people,
　　　　the Lord praise yee.

Psalme 149.

PRaise yee the Lord: unto the Lord
　　doe yee sing a new song:
　　& in the congregation
　　　his praise the Saints among.

2　Let Israell now joyfull bee
　　in him who him hath made:
　children of Sion in their King
　　o let them be full glad.

3　O let them with *melodious* flute
　　his Name give praise unto:
　let them sing praises unto him
　　with Timbrell, Harp also.

4　Because Iehovah in his folk
　　doth pleasure greatly take:
　the meek bee with salvation
　　ev'n beautifull will make.

5　Let them the gracious Saints that be
　　most gloriously rejoyce:
　& as they lye upon their beds
　　lift up their singing voyce.

6 Let their mouths have Gods praise: their hand
   a two edg'd sword also:

7 On heathen vengeance, on the folk
   punishment for to do:

8 Their kings with chaines, with yron bolts
   also their peers to binde:

9 To doe on them the judgement writ:
   all's Saints this honour finde.
                         Hallelujah.

Psalme 150.

PRaise yee the Lord, praise God
   in's place of holines:
 o praise him in the firmament
   of his great mightines.

2 O praise him for his acts
   that be magnificent:
 & praise yee him according to
   his greatnes excellent.

3 With Trumpet praise yee him
   that gives a sound so hye:
 & doe yee praise him with the Harp,
   & sounding Psalterye.

4 With Timbrell & with Flute
   praise unto him give yee:
 with Organs, & string'd instruments
   prais'd by you let him bee.

5 Vpon the loude Cymbals
   unto him give yee praise:
 upon the Cimballs praise yee him
   which hye their sound doe raile.

6 Let every thing to which
the Lord doth breath afford
the praises of the Lord set forth:
o doe yee praise the Lord.

FINIS

An admonition to the Reader.

THe verses of these psalmes may be reduced to
six kindes, the first wherof may be sung in very neere fourty common tunes; as they are col-
lected, out of our chief musicians, by *Tho. Ravers-
croft.*

The second kinde may be sung in three tunes as
Pf. 25. 50. & 67. in our english psalm books.

The third. may be sung indifferently, as *pf.* the 51.
100. & ten comandements, in our english psalme
books. which three tunes aforesaid, comprehend
almost all this whole book of psalmes, as being
tunes most familiar to us.

The fourth. as *pf.* 148. of which there are but a-
bout five.

The fift. as *pf.* 112. or the *Pater noster*, of which
there are but two. *viz.* 85. & 138.

The sixt. as *pf.* 113. of which but one, *viz.* 115.

Faults escaped in printing.

Escaped.	Right
psalme 9. vers 9. oprest.	opprest.
v. 10. knowes.	know.
ps. 18. u. 29. the.	thee.
u. 31. 3 part wanting.	3 part.
ps. 19. u. 13. let thou-	kept back
kept back.	o let.
ps. 21 u. 8. the Lord.	thine hand.
ps. 143. u. 6. seuen I.	moreover I.

The rest, which have escaped through over-
sight, you may amend, as you finde
them obvious.

Notes on the Reproduction

The process used for the production of this facsimile of the Bay Psalm Book of 1640 was line offset, with negatives made from an original copy of the Prince Collection in the Boston Public Library (No. 3 of the list printed in *The Enigma of the Bay Psalm Book*, p. 82). The pages were photographed, in exact size, by precision cameras in the shop of the Meriden Gravure Company at Meriden, Connecticut. Since the original copy, like all extant copies, contains a number of poorly printed pages, it seemed desirable to reproduce such pages from the second copy of the Prince Collection (No. 4 of the list).

The first facsimile of the Bay Psalm Book, published in 1903, was produced from the incomplete copy belonging to E. Dwight Church and now in the Huntington Library, using also the Lenox copy of the New York Public Library. In his Introduction, Wilberforce Eames, the foremost American bibliographer of his time, did not specify the pages prepared from the Lenox copy, mentioning as such only the first three leaves of the Preface. Yet the noting of substitutions may be useful. In the present facsimile the following pages were photographed from the second Prince copy: **v, A4v, F2, O3, S4, S4v, Tv, V3v (catchword retained from the first copy), V4, Aa, Aav, Aa2v, Aa4, Cc, Cc4v, Dd2, Dd2v, Ee, Eev, Ff4v, Ii3, Ll2. The catchwords of pages **2, D4, and R3v were also taken from the second Prince copy.

The presswork of the Bay Psalm Book was very uneven; Stephen Day at times thinned out the ink and at others splashed it over the forme, causing blotches and strong show-through. He probably never washed his type; signs of dried ink stuck between the letters are conspicuous throughout the book. The wet sheets must have attracted dust; and the fox-marks seem to have favored the edges of the letters as if the type, crushing the fiber of the paper, had rendered such areas especially sensitive. In making the present facsimile, these blemishes have been removed by careful opaquing, without retouching the negatives otherwise.

The earlier facsimile was produced from line cuts, that is, from plates prepared by etching; and, because of inept handling and the sponginess of the paper, the letters spread and became flat and heavy. No effort seems to have been made to clear the print of the ancient dirt. In contrast, the new facsimile has remarkable freshness and vitality.

Bibliographers may have preferred the reproduction of a single copy, with all its shortcomings, by the collotype process. The inclusion of the weak, barely legible, pages undoubtedly would have better revealed the quality of Day's printing. But even then only the characteristics of a particular copy would have been shown; for each copy has its own peculiar defects. It would have been unwarranted, therefore, to spoil the interest of the book for all but a few specialized scholars who can always examine the original copies. Still less could be said for perpetuating the damage wrought by time and usage.

The proofs were compared, letter by letter, with the original pages. For the correctness of the reproduction the writer testifies.

ZOLTÁN HARASZTI

BOSTON, MASSACHUSETTS
August 1956